JUDGEMENT

Judgement

BARRY COLLINS

FABER AND FABER
3 Queen Square
London

First published in 1974
by Faber and Faber Limited
3 Queen Square London WC1
Printed in Great Britain by
Whitstable Litho
All rights reserved

ISBN 0 571 10649 8

All rights in this play are reserved to the Proprietor.
All applications for professional and amateur rights
should be addressed to Spokesmen, 1 Craven Hill,
London, W2 3EW.

'Only a party to a case can really judge, but, being a party, it cannot judge. Hence there is no possibility of judgement in the world but only the glimmer of a possibility.' (Kafka)

CAST:

The Speaker - Andrei Vukhov, a Russian Army captain.
The Audience - as Judges.

NOTE:

The man, Vukhov, is a fiction; so, broadly, is the story
he tells. Certain details, however, are factual: they
relate to an episode of the Second World War. The
location was a hilltop monastery in southern Poland.
What happened there is described, briefly, in
George Steiner's <u>The Death of Tragedy</u>. Abandoning
the monastery, the Germans left a number of captured
Russian officers locked in a cellar. Two of the
prisoners managed to stay alive by killing and devouring
their companions. Eventually, the survivors were found
- crazed - by the advancing Red Army. First, they were
given a decent meal, then they were shot, 'lest the
soldiers see to what abjection their former officers had
been reduced' (Steiner). Afterwards, the monastery was
destroyed. Vukhov's monologue is a re-imagination of
the monastery incident, based on the premise that one of
the survivors was sane. Standing, as it were, 'in white
hospital tunic and regulation-issue slippers', he faces
the audience...

SPEAKER:

Comrades, I can see that I disgust you. My composure,
I think, revolts you: my ... normality. Forgive me: I
understand your distaste. I know I cannot expect your
pity. But then, I do not seek your pity. I see your pity
turns instead upon my brother, Rubin. That, too, I
understand. I would have it so. Yet, lacking your pity,
I must look to my defence - should you permit it. And
since you judge rather than pity me (I see it, comrades,
in your eyes, your ... impatience), I think you can hardly
deny me my defence. For my part, I am content to be
judged: I see my protection in your judgement, not your
pity .... May I enter, then, a plea of guilty? But of
course! How could I not be guilty in such a case? I am
guilty, I assure you. Then why a defence? Comrades,
excuse the irregularity: I propose to defend my guilt.
If you will allow it, I shall even bring a witness to my
guilt - a silent witness.... My irony offends you. I
apologise: I withdraw it. But I cannot, now, withdraw
my witness. Forgive me: it is the thighbone of Officer
Lubianko - to be precise, the left thighbone - sharpened,
you will note, to a point - on the stone floor of our cell
- for the purpose of killing Officer Rubin - my brother,
Rubin - I confess it - for killing comrade Officer Rubin,
at our eventual moment of trial - had it come to that -
between him and me - Rubin and Vukhov - the two last of

11

our seven.... At that moment, that final moment, could I have destroyed him? You will ask. I ask myself. Could I have done it? And I know I cannot tell. How can I tell what I would have done? How can we ever tell?... Please, I beg you, disregard my last question. Strike it out. I discuss no generalities. The history is mine: for me alone the question. Most certainly not for you. How could I presume to ask what you would have done? The problem is: what would I have done? And I admit, I do not know. There are, however, certain facts I can offer for your consideration. For example, that I joined readily, in full reason, in the death of Officer Tretyakov - Colonel Tretyakov that was.... Comrades! I see it: you are astonished - that I, a captain merely - Captain Vukhov, Andrei Vukhov, Captain Andrei Vukhov, tank squadron, third assault brigade - that I, Vukhov, should willingly have shared in the death of a superior, a comrade and brother. Nonetheless it was so: I conceal nothing - though you can have only my word for that, since Officer Rubin is no longer himself. Which, I suppose, might appear to introduce another fact, were it not a matter of opinion - I mean my brother Rubin's state of mind.... Since our deliverance, you have kept comrade Rubin asleep, in a closed room - his body bound, his spirit screened. Permit me, in exchange for one dungeon you confine him to another - still darker - by which I conclude you consider him to have lost his reason. Such, it would seem are the judgements of pity. After the torment Officer Rubin has undergone, I myself might assess his present state of mind differently - were I able, that is, to know his state of mind.... In the matter of my own mind, I gladly leave you to judge, as best you can. And be assured, I sympathise - since you must decide
12

what shall be done with me.... For the purpose, as I
say, you will need certain facts. And they are these -
principally these: that I and six comrade officers,
captured in the enemy counter-offensive along salient
fourteen, were entombed in a cell in the abandoned
monastery of St. Peter Rabinovich on 23rd May - a cell
measuring eleven paces long by nine paces wide and some
twenty feet high - and that in this cell, without food or
water, my brothers and I remained for more than two
months, until the enemy was pushed back yet again and
we were released - that is, Officer Rubin and I, the two
survivors.... Comrades, surely you cannot miss the
paradox here, the paradox we two present. Perhaps
you would term it something else, something less neutral,
but I prefer the paradox - of Major Rubin's insanity, as
you conceive it, and my ... composure. No, I thought
not. Your suspicions are evident. Am I, then, sane,
who marshal my thoughts, my words, as you do: who can
muster reason to defend obscenities that should strike
reason dumb? I see that my own state of mind, in your
assessment, is my accuser. And with that, too, I am
content. I am not as I should be, you feel. How can it
be that I am so composed? I am not as Officer Rubin,
whom you judge deranged, therefore I am twice an
obscenity. Is it not so?... Forgive me, comrades: I
am what I am. Upon your ... paradox, all I would say is
that, at the last, my brother Rubin's state of mind
allowed me some advantage over him, and, had we not
been, as it were, disinterred, I should have had to
decide upon employment of that advantage - or otherwise.
For by the eighth week - yes, the eighth week - I kept
the days most carefully, comrades - by the sun - since

we were stripped of our effects, stripped of everything,
left naked, when the enemy imprisoned us - stripped even
of our uniforms - a cruel touch that, I think, to take our
uniforms, in the circumstances ... however, by the sun
- entering and leaving our cell each day, through a small
barred window, high on the outer wall - by the sun, I say,
I, at least, kept time, kept strict time - and by the eighth
week, when we were alone, he and I, the last two, the
survivors - Officer Rubin was much changed. His
strength remained - much greater strength than mine (he
was a gymnast, let me tell you, in his respites from the
war). But he sobbed so: he wept and moaned and
screamed by turns, he babbled like a child and tore his
hair and clawed his skin; he clawed a hole in his side
- with his fingernails - and another in his neck. Doubtless your doctors have noticed them - deep holes,
festering.... Sometimes he slept, quite unguardedly.
And then I would leave my wall and go to him, to nurse
him, to cradle him.... You doubt me: I see it, comrades.
You remember my witness: I am glad you remember it
- the piece of bone, the sharpened thighbone, poor
Lubianko's thighbone - you remember it and you ask: are
we to believe, then, that a man who has already prepared
the means of his brother's death will yet nurse that same
brother as he lies, defenceless, in his arms? Or is it the
tenderness (may I call it so?), the tenderness ... is it the
tenderness itself you cannot accept - at such an extremity?
Do you perhaps consider me incapable of tenderness? ...
No! No! That question, too, is unworthy. Forgive me:
it must be enough for me to say that in the days of my
brother Rubin's pain, I cradled him in his sleep, and
would hold him, then, until he woke, a little clearer, less
distraught, and would throw me aside - back to my wall
14

- in fear, you understand, at his own unguardedness -
only to begin his weeping again, a moment later. I even
fed him.... Oh, come now, comrades! Yes! I fed him!
Your horror, it is not reasonable. I reject it. Be frank:
what hope have I, of you, in such horror? How do you
think we were still alive, Officer Rubin and I, after sixty
days? I fed him, comrades, as I fed myself - on the flesh
of our dead brothers. And your horror at that feeding,
your shrinking from it, they do you no credit, here, in
this wide room, as my judges. If the story were new to
you, if you had not heard it! But by now the whole army
must have heard it - such a monstrous story could not
easily be hidden. Why, then, this horror at hearing it
again, from me? Unless it is me, personally, you find so
horrifying.... Comrades, I declare: your horror is not
real, it is formal - it is the revulsion not of reason but of
sentiment. If you judge me, haven't I the right, at least,
to your reason? The emotion of horror I would grant only
to Officer Scriabin - presumably you have read his report:
I shall spare you repetition - but to Scriabin alone I would
concede horror - to the young lieutenant of infantry who
broke open the door of our prison and in the beam of his
torch saw me feeding my brother Rubin, saw me feeding
him the flesh of another man - and saw the remains of our
dead comrades.... But you, my judges, have seen nothing.
You have only heard: it is only words you hear, words
you recoil from - and if these words revolt you the more
because they are my words - because my words are
composed and clear, the words of knowing, not of rumour
and report - if these words disgust you, then you have
judged me already in your hearts and such judgement
brings shame as much upon you as it brings upon me.
Before suffer that judgement, I would beg the pity you have

15

shown to Officer Rubin. For my brother Rubin, could he
speak of it, would say you have heard little yet. And how
can you judge without proper hearing? Surely you did not
think to avoid a proper hearing?... Or perhaps you
suspect I seek to spread my guilt by speaking it? Not at
all, comrades: I am unrepresentative: I require no
excuse: I would be content to carry my guilt, alone,
among you. But you, forgive me, would not have it so.
You would make some decision, some ruling upon me.
And I accept that. Comrades, I accept your need -
correction, your duty - to judge me: I submit to it: I
know the questions you must try to answer. Oh yes,
comrades, I appreciate your perplexity. You wonder
how a sane man could return whole, as it were, from
such an experience. You examine Officer Rubin
- washed clean, now, of all that filth and blood, his hair
shorn, and his beard, his bowels sealed, his wounds
dressed - and you know that if he woke he would be wild:
he would cower against the wall, more like an animal
than a man, you would say, with his fingers crooked,
his tongue lolling, and he would howl and howl and howl...
so you bind him down, comrades, in his closed white
cubicle, with thick straps at the arms and legs, and you
keep him asleep, you keep him from his own mind -
because you pity the terror you think it brings him. You
consider him mad, and his madness authentic, a healthy
reaction - forgive the irony - to his torment. Yet
because his wildness is unseemly, because he would be a
danger, loose, to himself and to others, you anaesthetise
him to a cleanly calm, you restore him, as it were, to his
lost humanity by making him a breathing corpse. And if
you held him there long enough, comrades, you might
almost forget the tale he cannot tell - except you know
16

there is such fear, such agony locked within that quiet sleep, and you wonder, sometimes 'Does he dream?' and you think, perhaps, to put him out of his misery. But should you do that - should you presume to do it - what, then, would you do with me, who am not noticeably miserable? Or, lacking that presumption, would you keep my brother Rubin estranged from his new self until he should die, as it were, naturally? And in that case, again, comrades, what would be done with me? Would I, too, be set apart? From myself? I need no such protection. From others? Forgive me - I would ask: upon what grounds? Am I not fit for return to the war? Am I otherwise than normal? Less than human? Examine me, comrades. Allowing the customary effects of such incarceration - a yellowing of the skin, a certain weakness of the chest and limbs, a tendency to stoop, a certain frailty of the bladder - I think I function normally enough, in the circumstances. And why not? It is remarkable, comrades, what the human system can absorb, the human frame subsist upon. Considered objectively (that is to say, dietetically) many men have fed far worse than I and yet survived.... You couldn't believe one man's flesh would rot another's innards, that one man's blood would stop another's veins. That would be superstition, wouldn't it? My body argues so. Were I to father a child at this moment, I think its birth - other things being equal - would not prove monstrous.... Even that horrifies you, comrades. Perhaps especially that. You make no pretence of your horror. At what? That I should still feel such ordinary desires? My pulse is steady, my temperature regular - my heart is sound. By any medical test, I am, I suggest, only marginally unhealthy. Am I, then, to be kept from my wife and

17

children? Restrained? Quarantined? To prevent
contamination? Or am I as normal as I seem - unusual
only in what I have experienced?... You see, comrades,
I recognise your dilemma - as I borrow your categories.
Am I to return to your soldier-community - at my present
rank and command? If so, you must wonder, what might
be the effect upon discipline, upon morale? My
compatriots, comrades, how would they receive me?
Violently? With loathing? Or with pity, or disdain
- perhaps with alarm?... Can I be trusted, comrades?
What of my courage, my resilience, my response to
action? You cannot be sure: I am no longer ...
predictable. Should I, then, be dismissed? Should I be
transferred to other duties in some far corner of the war
- administration, possibly? And if so, upon what grounds,
forgive me, could I be excused the conflict in which my
brothers are called, day after day, to give their very
lives? Indeed, upon what considerations, what
distinctions of normality - or otherwise - are my
brothers themselves consigned to their various fronts,
their theatres of this war?... Your pardon, comrades:
the question is rhetorical, of course: it exceeds the
bounds of my legitimate concern - that is, myself - my
own case. It is to you, comrades, that detachment, in
this matter, must belong.... How, precisely, am I
changed? Am I, so to speak, of any further use?...
Comrades, I understand, these problems can hardly be
avoided.... But first, and above all, I suppose, the
question of my present composure: is it merely a skin,
beneath which those dreadful days still boil? How have I
escaped when my brother Rubin has been so hurt? May it
not be that I have escaped unfairly? Am I not correct?
You suspect me of a certain ... criminality: you must
18

interrogate me, must put my experience to the test of
your laws, your codes, your judgement, which judgement
you seek to extend, without limit, to all things human and,
heretofore, divine.... Very well, comrades, I am
prepared: I concede that I must earn my return to
customary society - that is, forgive me, to the war - by
establishing my fitness for the war. But you judge my
present fitness, it seems, only by judging my recent
experience. Therefore, I maintain you must hear the
facts of that experience. Is it not so? I almost said 'the
truth' of my experience. Absurd! Rather, the facts.
The truth of my facts is for you to assess. So I beg you,
comrades - hear me. Listen with your stomachs, if you
will, with your noses and your tongues, your teeth, if
you must, even listen, yes with your hearts, but at least,
comrades, listen.... Do me that service, please - to
hear what I tell and remember it, as you judge me. In
turn, I can perhaps offer certain preliminary details
- verifiable details, I think - to encourage your trust in
my accuracy.... Colonel Tretyakov, for instance, had
a wife with only one breast, who fed her fourth child
upon that one breast, solely, without undue discomfort....
Again I shock you, comrades! Such mundanity - in the
circumstances - it disturbs you. But I wonder, in your
own experience, what do men do when imprisoned together?
Don't they talk - at first? And at first, don't they talk of
themselves and their families? So Officer Tretyakov
spoke of his wife - to me - yes, to a subordinate - he
spoke to me of his wife's deformity. Similarly, I spoke
to him of my wife - the little toe on her right foot is
missing, as it happens, and she has a scar on her throat,
which she tries to hide by keeping her hair long.... It
is not unusual, I think - Officer Lysenko spoke of the

19

death of his mother ... Officer Lysenko, comrades.
Lysenko. Major Lysenko: tank squadron, third assault
brigade. You have the names, I presume - the seven
names. Officer Tretyakov, Officer Lysenko, Officer
Lubianko, Officer Banishevsky, Officer Blok, Officer
Rubin and myself - Vukhov, Andrei Vukhov. Seven men,
in rank from colonel - Tretyakov, to company sergeant
- Banishevsky ... Lev Alexandrovich Banishevsky,
comrades - we grew up together, he and I: we were boys
together in Ryazan: we joined the war together, fought
through four retreats and three offensives together - he
had been decorated after the fifth, no, the sixth battle
for the very monastery - St. Peter Rabinovich - where
we were imprisoned.... And this friend - yes,
comrades - this childhood friend, this dearest of
brothers - I gnawed his flesh, yes, I tore at his body, I
sucked his bones - yes comrades! Your horror, it
revolts me: it is so predictable - you savour it! Is
this a judgement or an entertainment? Must I accommodate
my experience to your feelings as well as to your scales,
your rules, your measures of behaviour? You have a
chart, have you - a graph - a checklist, against which
you can range my testimony, ticking off my evidence
against your categories, to calculate the degree of my
residual humanity? And in your categories, comrades,
tell me, does the flesh of a friend taste worse, less
wholesome, than that of a mere acquaintance, a brother
officer, compatriot and fellow prisoner?... Perhaps you
will allow me to suggest certain new categories for your
list. For example, I might detail, in order of preference,
the choicest regions of the human anatomy.... Oh yes,
comrades, do not doubt it! How could you possibly doubt
it? One develops one's likes and dislikes in such a case,
20

as in any other. Shall it be loin, do you think, or thigh?
Kidneys - or liver? Come now, comrades, do not shrink!
Remember: listen with your tongues! Shall I tell you how
long it takes six men to tear another man to pieces, using
only their teeth and fingernails? Shall I tell you why
genitals tend to be left late (in such a case) and heads
left quite alone? Does blood taste better warm or cold,
comrades? Shall I tell you? Shall I report my own
findings? I am a connoisseur of sorts in these matters.
Shall I help you feel the slip of human entrails? Shall I
discriminate, for your information, between the eating of
human excrement and the eating of human flesh, ex-
plaining why the latter might be preferred at a certain
stage of our entombment? ... Surely my findings will prove
valuable: surely you will welcome such rare data?
Might you not even honour me for it? Am I not a
traveller returned from a lost frontier? Am I not
amplifying your present measure of man: am I not
broadening the scales you seek to weigh me in? Am I not,
in fact, a hero: the man who has come through - the
survivor? And might I not, therefore, lay some claim to
your admiration: might I not deserve a decoration: am I
not a walking testimony to the effectiveness of our basic
survival training? ... Perhaps not - when my six
brothers - five now dead and one asleep - all graduated
by the same course as I.... Were we victims, then, of
some fate beyond the manual of basic training? Yes,
comrades - victims! Should I play the victim? Should I
fall to my knees before you, asking how I have offended
God, that he could have done this to me - or bewailing
the monstrous, alien universe in which we all suffer so
terribly, so incomprehensibly, and of which suffering my
own suffering is part, and me your exemplar in such

suffering? Should I enter a complaint, comrades, an existential complaint, saying I did not ask to be shut, without sustenance, for sixty days, in a cell with six others? Comrades, should I say it wasn't my fault? Should I embellish my story with fine language, mythologise myself - a latter-day Ulysses, my prison another dark island on that journey of doubtful genesis and uncertain conclusion? Should I pluck at your heart-strings with the anguish of my sojourn in the blackest recesses of the human soul? Should I tell the piteous moments of my brothers' several deaths and tell them piteously, with suitable tokens of my grief? Yes, comrades: shall I compile a new prayer book of their lamentations? Shall I give you touching proof of their compassion for each other at the very farthest reaches of their suffering? Shall I detail comfort - and cowardice - by name and serial number?... Or should I stay silent? Is that it, comrades, is that what you want: that I should stay silent, after all? This mouth, it is the mouth of a cannibal.... Of course, comrades, a cannibal! I would be the first to state the fact. And when the facts are so terrible, why such terror at a mere word?... Very well, let us say, instead, that I was reduced to the most hideous savagery: if I was so ... reduced, then that darkness must remain, somewhere within me. How can I speak of my case without betraying it? So shouldn't I stay quiet - pretend that suffering has shrivelled my tongue, or my memory? Should I pretend my story is so horrible that I cannot bear the telling of it, or even summon the words to match it? Should I perhaps lock my story fast inside myself - to spare you all the thought of what the war has made of me? Is that what you want: is that what you demand of me - the courtesy of

keeping quiet, of sparing you the enormity of what I have
to tell?... Really, comrades: it cannot be - in fairness
to myself. Don't you already have the evidence of the
young lieutenant of infantry, Officer Scriabin, who found
my brother Rubin and I - and freed us? To remain silent
after such testimony would be to condemn myself before
you. Comrades, let me remind you: I spoke to Scriabin,
and having once spoken, silence, for me, became
impossible. The silence was for my brother Rubin - at
least, the lack of words - and now you seek to perfect
his silence. But for me, the moment I gave sign of
rationality, it became necessary to defend that
rationality. And I remember it - the exact moment - the
precise sequence of moments.... It was night: the
sixtieth night - only faint moonlight through the high
grille - and suddenly the sound of footsteps beyond the
door, the sudden vaulting of my heart, the shock,
comrades, my ears pricking like a dog's, my breath
caught, not thinking to shout, to intervene, my body
rigid in attention - the shock, I say, comrades,
commingled already with regret - dismay even - a
fractional dismay, that it was over, that the pattern had
changed again, that a new pattern would be needed....
Extraordinary, comrades, the dismay of breached resignation - disappointment, almost, at a trial postponed, a
trial I had accepted - and still resisted - whose stages I
had anticipated and understood, a trial now cut short, to
my dismay - and the dismay mingling with the shock, the
hope, then swallowed by it - all in an instant - swallowed
by the joy, the exaltation of my life reopening, vast,
without horizons, briefly, as the bolts were drawn, the
locks were smashed and the door, the great iron door,
cracked open at Officer Scriabin's shoulder, his breath

coming in gasps from the effort as the hinges split with a noise like thunder after all that silence, and his cry of revulsion - I remember it - he must have turned aside for a second at the reek of us - then his torchlight - a torch, comrades, just a torch, a torchlight sweeping quickly round the cell, my brother Rubin cowering, panic-stricken in my arms and yelping, and the torch veering towards the noise and still taking an age to reach it - an age - then passing us, returning, fixing us, freezing my brother Rubin in my arms - like a child in my arms, and I, blinded - even my eyes, sharper than a cat's in all that darkness, blinded, in a torch, and the torchlight merciless, unwavering, and I, relaxing in its beam, lying back, without shame, against the wall, flooded with calm, a century of calm - expectant, shame-less.... And I knew, instantly, whoever he was - for I could not see him in the glare - I knew him as comrade, not enemy, and I knew the front must have moved to the west, along the riverline - the counter-attack had come to the west (which was why I had not heard the echo of the guns), and a flanking force had slipped along the valley and struck up through the birch forest, in a circling movement, and an infantry squad was checking the silent monastery ruins at the heart of the sweep - the abandoned monastery - I understood it all instantly.... The young lieutenant said only: 'Oh, my God!' which was as serviceable a phrase as any, I think, in the circum-stances - and at the very same moment, I said: 'At last! You must have struck north through the birch forest' - I remember it - the precise words - and I felt him stiffen, I felt him recoil, over there, at the far end of the torch-light, in the broken doorway, and again I understood, immediately: I saw what he saw, through his eyes - as
24

the beam held me, I saw what it told him, I saw us, Rubin
and me, transfixed in the light, and I was already weeping, uncontrollably weeping, in shame, in relief, in fear,
in weakness - and holding my brother Rubin the closer as
I wept.... And then the torchlight moved from us; it
began to seek out the cell; I watched it move and fix,
and move and fix; and I saw again what Scriabin saw, I
saw the cell as I had never seen it, with someone else's
eyes - the high walls, the carpet of blood, like moss,
the ... remains, the row of heads - oh, the row of heads
- how reverently Rubin had placed them, those heads,
five heads in a row, solemnly, their eyelids closed,
their faces to the wall, as solemn, as private, to us, as
undisturbed, as in a tomb, a brotherly tomb - but to him,
the young lieutenant, unspeakably horrifying.... And the
torch moved back to us in the cool darkness, questioning
- the young lieutenant tried to ask who we were: were we
his, he meant, were we his? And I said: 'Yes'. 'Yes',
I said, 'yes, yes, we're yours. Captain Vukhov, Major
Rubin. We're yours! We're yours!'... And from those
moments, comrades - perhaps you can appreciate -
silence, for me, was no recourse. If I am to return to the
war, I must make my own report - I know that - even if
only for your files. And in truth, I don't doubt there are
words enough for the purpose: words, that is, to say
what is sayable - to tell you what you need to know -
about our ... cannibalism.... Indeed, comrades, I
repeat it: I, at least, suffer no crisis of identity: the
dictionary itself defines me cannibal - yes, cannibal - a
cannibal in hospital tunic and size ten regulation-issue
slippers.... Pending your judgement, it seems, I am
still denied my uniform.... When your young lieutenant,
Scriabin, freed us from our prison, Rubin and me, he

25

sent back for two greatcoats, to cover us - which was typical of his thoughtfulness, his command of the situation.... Barefoot, in a borrowed greatcoat, I walked upright, and quite steadily, from our tomb, without a pause, a backward glance, a mark of respect, remembrance, farewell. Doubtless the good lieutenant recalled the fact.... Oh, but I ask you, comrades, am I likely to foget that room, that stone room: did I need a last glance, did I need any farewell? Your lieutenant appropriated our cell the second he shone his torch upon it. And the moment we were gone, he blew it up - again, I think, a commendable decision: he closed the door upon the remains of our dead brothers and, while Officer Rubin and myself were being taken back down through the birch forest, he dynamited what was left of the monastery - the underground chambers, the passages, the fountains, the tower.... But, comrades, I carry that cell within me, as it was in the sixty days before Scriabin broke the seal upon it - and I carried that cell within me as I left, barefoot, in a borrowed greatcoat, climbing the spiral steps towards the light, my feet, in the darkness, seeking the shallow imprints of a thousand years of holy men.... When we crossed the lines, below the birch forest, the greatcoat was taken from me - and burned. I was given my white tunic, my regulation slippers, and left alone, isolate, observed - needing little medicine and no psychiatry, and therefore, I suspect, invested with imaginary deformities. A hump, perhaps? Or fangs?... Examine me, comrades, I say: apply your customary standards. Am I not normal? A normal cannibal: a cannibal well read in the classics, trained as an engineer, versed in the relativity theory and the second law of thermodynamics, familiar with the atom,

aware that the flesh I ate was all but nothing, almost
without substance, that my brothers' souls registered no
taste whatsoever.... In other words, am I not the
logical savage, compelled to justify my savagery because
I can explain it? Comrades, my explanation shall be my
defence! I am content to state the facts - as I saw
them.... Of course, it is possible you might trust my
evidence the more should I savour it with contrition,
should I exhibit an intolerable weight of guilt....
Comrades, even I could not trust such demonstrations!
In any case, I feel no guilt. Believe me, I say so
without bravado. I recognise the certainty of my guilt,
yet I do not feel it - and, for once, I see no paradox
here. Since there can be no innocence in such a case,
there must be guilt - your categories insist upon it. The
only issue, I think, is what must be done with me: the
single courtesy I would ask would be some statement of
the nature of my guilt. Conceding my guilt, of what am
I guilty? What, precisely, have I done, that should bar
me from your own society and from the war?... For
myself, as I stand before you, in my heart (if you will
permit me such simplicities) I cannot find my guilt: I
feel no contrition, no terrible remorse: I feel neither
pity nor self-pity. I feel the residue of many emotions
which were once real but I no longer feel their reality....
Then what do I feel?... Comrades, my defence is what I
feel.... Comrades, I feel - alive!... Forgive me, I
cannot entirely ... explain what I feel. Standing before
you, I say, certain regions of my mind seem numb, as if
... cauterised.... My memory, however, is clear, I
believe, my faculties unimpaired. Therefore, I present
my report to you without embellishment, with what
precision I can command - the report of our entombment.

27

And, comrades, may I not claim, now, that this is the only
duty I owe you in the matter: to report the occurrence as
I might have reported any other occurrence of the war?
For was this not as much a wartime occurrence as our
heroic autumn drive upon salient seven? An act of war,
comrades, only an act of war, and I an actor in that
war - Captain Vukhov, comrades, Captain Andrei Vukhov,
tank squadron, third assault brigade, begging to report
an episode of war, 23rd May to 22nd July, at the
monastery of St. Peter Rabinovich, bordering Katowice,
southern Poland.... Brothers, fellow combatants: at
first there seemed nothing unusual in our imprisonment,
except perhaps the nakedness, which I have mentioned
- the nakedness was ... unnerving.... We were not
unaware of certain, shall I say, irregularities, occurring
on our own side of the hostilities, and, knowing how the
war had degenerated, of late, we waited, at least, for
interrogation. We had no casualities - it had been a
disaster, a rout: we just waited, quietly, demoralised,
uncertain - for twelve hours, I would guess.... No one
came near, with questions or with food. Then suddenly
- it must have been about dawn - the enemy noved out - and
left us. There was a great commotion, comrades, engines
roaring, hatches closing, commands, tramping feet on the
cobbles of the courtyard, high above, outside the little
window. Then everything was silent.... Eventually,
someone - it must have been the colonel - suggested we
build a pyramid, to try and reach the high grille.
Officer Rubin, may I say, once the gymnast, proved the
pivot of this exercise - ungainly as it was. And after
several calamities (we made lacklustre acrobats),
Officer Blok, being smallest of the seven, was hoisted up
to the bars, where he managed only the briefest

observation across the courtyard before the pyramid
collapsed, with much attendant bruising, not least to
Officer Blok himself, who was left hanging perilously
from the window grille for a second or so before falling
heavily into the pile of bodies beneath, with a quite
consummate death-howl - all of which caused great
merriment, and a momentary relief of tension.... There
was even something faintly hilarious, at that instant, in
what he had seen. We lay there, crumpled in a heap,
gasping with laughter, and Officer Blok, between gasps,
said: 'They've gone: they've all gone.' And I
remember, distinctly, we began to laugh again, on reflex,
perhaps ... then slowly the laughter drifted away. We
couldn't understand it. The monastery of St. Peter: we
had fought and counter-fought for it, month by month,
through the snow and early spring - the chapels, the
cloisters, the huge granaries were all in ruins, the
dormitories destroyed - only the tower remained
remotely whole, above ground, after all that fighting
- and now the enemy had moved out, only twelve hours
after recapturing it. Officer Blok was quite specific:
there was no sign of life outside. The defeat must have
been more ruinous than we had imagined: already, the
artillery seemed far away - only an echo, the faintest
echo, beyond the ridge.... Up to that point, no one had
bothered about the door - an enormous iron door, set
deep in the wall. Now we all had the same thought:
'What about us?' - all at the same time. It was uncanny:
the laughter drained away and we were all looking at the
door - the iron door - wondering (I know it): 'What about
us?'... Naturally, Colonel Tretyakov was the one to find
out. I remember, comrades, he was limping a little - his
leg had been twisted in the fall.... He walked across to

29

the door, examined it, found it fast and solid, felt in the
wall-surround, stood a moment, with his back to us - his
narrow, white back - then turned and said, rather flatly,
I thought: 'It's locked' - just, 'It's locked' - with an odd
smile at the corner of his mouth.... The cell itself was
obvious - like a water cistern, cut from the rock. There
was just that tiny hole, high up, beneath the roof.
Officer Blok said the window bars were firm: the
opening was much too small, even for him. The cell
floor was stone, not quite smooth, not quite perfect, for
all its wearing.... At the beginning, we had sat - or
lain - casually, together, in the centre: now, curiously,
we all moved back against the walls, separate: we were
waiting on the colonel - his assessment. 'There could
be several explanations,' he said, finally: 'We must
wait, that's all'.... Later, several days later, I
suggested we should keep definite track of time.... It
was about noon on the eleventh day, by my count, that
Officer Tretyakov proposed drawing lots.... Personally,
I could never believe the enemy had simply left us: even
towards the end, I still suspected it might be some
ghastly experiment. We have not been averse to certain
... experiments of our own, I know, comrades - and I
felt, somehow, we might be ... under observation:
right to the last, I felt sure they would come back,
eventually, to check the results ... and I do not know
whether it was worse or better that they didn't ... that
they never intended to - or did they? - that they merely
left us - to ourselves .... We drank our own wine,
then our own sperm; we sucked our own blood - we
queued and climbed to ease our withering mouths on
the damp rock around the grille .... It was hopeless.
Day by day, at different rates, we all passed through
30

the various stages of crisis - thirst, hunger, pain, rage, acceptance, delirium, despair.... Not surprisingly, some retained more control than others: it is a question of constitution, comrades, as well as a question of will. What frailties there were among us - or rather, what precise varieties of reaction - I cannot possibly suggest without implying some judgement, some criterion for judgement of my brothers. And who, comrades, could presume to judge another, in such a case, without knowing him, absolutely, his entire life, his experience, his medical history, his descent - which would be difficult, at best, don't you agree?... Personally, I know nothing, remember nothing, that might, in my own eyes, impeach any of my dead companions. And I would hope to say nothing that might impeach them in your different eyes. Nor shall I speak of my brother Rubin, except where my care for the facts makes it reasonable - and then only, in my own estimation, to do him honour. I can speak with justice simply of myself - insofar as I know myself. And, for myself, I can speak of the most ungovernable panics, the most demeaning fears and fantasies, the most grovelling weakness - in those early days - when our situation was unclear - before it reached the extremity of some decision, before we attempted some strategy for ... endurance ... I was about to say, comrades, some strategy for survival: rather, for endurance - that is, before our decision to draw lots - with hair from our own heads - at our brother colonel's suggestion.... Until then (do you grasp the subtle refinement of taking our uniforms?), until then, Officer Tretyakov had been first, as it were, among equals, in our mutual nightmare; until then he had maintained the seniority of character ... 'the seniority of character.'

31

It rings glibly, comrades, doesn't it - at once too neat
and too vague? Forgive me. Let me say, rather that
despite everything, the colonel somehow kept a
chastening sense of care for his subordinates, and that,
through him, the gradations of rank proved, for a time,
some help - a structure, if you like, to contain our
suffering. Repeatedly, he reminded us that the
monastery had been seized, lost and seized again, in the
space of a single day, two summers before. Even if the
enemy had abandoned us, there remained the near-
certainty of a counter-offensive, he promised, then we
might be freed. For as long as he could, in fact, the
colonel insisted our position had not changed, that we
were simply combatants made prisoner. But finally,
this became impossible: the tensions, comrades -
perhaps you can imagine ... how we bayed, like animals,
below the window grille, how we scratched and scraped
our fingers raw upon the rock, the metal door ... finally,
I say, the tensions were unmanageable.... Twice we
fell to blows - certain of us - and in the second brawl,
one of us was bitten, quite badly, on the calf and shoulder
.... It was degrading, comrades ... battle-hardened
officers, interdependent, for our courage and skills, a
thousand times dependent for our very lives, now we
were turning against each other: officers who had
worried, constantly, at first, about their men - what had
happened to them, the dozens of men captured with us in
our massive defeat - now these same officers were baiting
and bullying each other, abusing one another - all the
resentments and jealousies of a graded society were
breaking free. Sleep itself had become fearful, fitful.
From our separate kingdoms along the four walls, we
watched the progress of each other's hysterias with
32

growing mistrust - and always, in that mistrust, a
fevered eye upon our own agonies, the secret fading of
our own parched flesh.... We were no longer
prisoners of the enemy: no longer prisoners of anyone:
prisoners only of the war - subject not to the great
conventions, only to the war's caprice. It was an
unfamiliar position: there had to be some decision of
response. And it could not be a decision by rank or
authority: if you will excuse the play on words, it could
only be a corporate decision. Officer Tretyakov knew
this: the unmentionable had to be discussed: we had to
reach some resolve before suffering carried things
beyond us.... It was like a staff meeting: I remember
it vividly. We all moved together again, into the centre
of the cell: the discussion was calm - at least,
relatively so. After the torments we had severally
undergone - torments of mind and body - torment,
comrades, of the cancelled soul - after such torments,
the act of coming back together was a great comfort, a
new means of control. And in the calm of that control,
we decided, together, that our only recourse (forgive me)
was for us each, in turn, to surrender our bodies to feed
our surviving brothers.... You are shocked, comrades
- no, I do you an injustice: you are amazed - if I may say
so - that such a course of action was selected rationally,
with due deliberation and accord. Nonetheless, I stress
it: despite the brawling, our decision was not one taken
in frenzy - not, at that point anyway, a decision of blood,
not even a case of the strong devouring the weak, no mere
matter of survival of the fittest.... Comrades, you
conjure with simplicities: you underestimate the degree
of selflessness the human animal can summon at such
extremities ... always provided a certain framework

33

remains, requiring common action, appealing to one's sense of interconnection.... Listen to me! Lecturing again - when I need only submit that, by acting soon enough, before the frame of loyalty finally broke, we hoped to anticipate, at least temporarily, the frenzy we all feared - to resist, as long as possible, what I have termed the war's caprice.... The actual result, you may suggest, was the same in reason as it would have been in frenzy. But in this war, wouldn't you agree, there is still something to be gained by preserving appearances? Since the war makes such vile demands upon us, wouldn't you say it is only in our manner of meeting those demands that we mark out the degree of our continuing humanity? Isn't this very hearing, the courtesy you extend me, comrades, in this very room, isn't this, too, just a way of keeping up appearances - of giving form to this particular theatre of the war? Let me tell you, comrades, that the choice between reason and frenzy was not, by any means, the most difficult of our decisions - and, once taken, and taken early enough, it was not, in the circumstances - speaking relatively, you understand - especially hard to pursue. No, the question which caused most heartsearching was whether we should attempt a strategy for endurance at all. Perhaps I may summarise the predicament: if the price, as it were, of staying alive a little longer was progressively to devour each other, then was the price of staying alive worth paying? Might it not better reflect our dignity as human beings to die together, in agreement, than to divide ourselves, so literally, in our agony? In other words, comrades - collective suicide.... You shudder: I see it - you almost ... disapprove! Our duty, you might say, was to endure - to ensure some element of survival, at

whatever cost, for as long as possible - in the event of a
change of fortune - a reversal of the military situation,
which might free us, or the surviving remnant of us, for
a return to the war.... Exactly, comrades - our own
sentiments exactly! Endurance is all! As a group, at
least, we decided that, on balance, endurance is all....
And you can have faint conception, I think, comrades,
what emotion that decision created within us - what
solidarity - what mutual awareness - what brotherhood
- what love.... Oh, what extraordinary gestures human
kind can make, collectively, even at such moments of
ultimate challenge! We felt we were giving ... dignity
to what would follow.... Upon reflection, how ridiculous!
What followed was merely appalling. How does one
preserve one's dignity in cleaning another man's bones?
Remember my witness, comrades, my silent witness: if
you will pardon a further generalisation - it says what
infinite capacity for self-delusion we humans also have.
The more intolerable the reality of this war, the more
we must preserve appearances - that is all! Appearances,
not dignity. Where is my dignity, that I must stand here
to defend myself in such an awful case? Where, comrades,
I ask you? In what am I dignified? Even now, I employ
only another strategy for survival - I admit it - here,
now, I seek to endure - that is all - to persuade you, by
reason, to permit my return to the war - and where is the
dignity in that?... Forgive me, comrades! Such
whining! Such pointless whining! It must be an
embarrassment to you: I apologise.... Let me say,
simply, that we, the seven of us, decided at the
eleventh day, to draw lots - to reckon ourselves - with
the hair of our own heads; that Officer Tretyakov
arranged and held the hairs, and, that, in the way such

35

things happen, the lot fell upon him - his own silvering
hair was the one he had broken, his own hair was the one
left in his hand when we had each drawn, in turn.... And
from that point onward, it seemed, our situation had a
new logic. We had even agreed on a method of despatch!
The brother selected by lot was to be smothered -
collectively: we wanted no executioners: the responsibility must be shared - in part for explanation, in the
event of our release, but principally, of course, to
spread the burden of the deed - in a sense (I see it now)
to ritualise the deed, to distance ourselves from it, if
that were possible, through ritual.... Officer Tretyakov
made no complaint when the lot fell upon him: there was
just that strange smile at the corner of his mouth. The
rest of us watched him, silently - relieved, frightened
.... Had the result been different - had someone else
been chosen...? Naturally you will wonder, comrades:
I have wondered myself. But the fact is that Colonel
Tretyakov was chosen. And, whatever his feelings, he
made no play of his seniority, in the sense either of
challenging or welcoming the reckoning. Gently, gravely,
he embraced us all, without distinction, as we sat
- kneeling to kiss each one of us, to whisper goodbye,
to speak hope and courage. Then he asked if he might
be allowed to sleep. He went back to his place on the
wall - opposite the door - knelt again, for a moment
(though I could not say whether he prayed), then asked us
to tell his wife - if any of us survived - that he thought of
her as he died, and quietly, he fell asleep.... Watching
him, from the centre of the cell, we were astonished,
strengthened - the pale, slight figure, curled like a
child, knees drawn up.... It was so - correct: an act
of ... love - to confirm us, I interpret, in what we must
36

do.... We waited, listening for the measure of his
breathing, then we moved, together, and, holding his
body firmly, we smothered him - our senior officer - with
our hands - covering his eyes, covering his whole face,
we ... extinguished him - like a candle - so softly, so
quickly: it took just a few seconds - he did not struggle
- only his body stiffened as he woke and remained taut a
little, then relaxed.... We held him much longer than
necessary - to make sure.... His beard, I remember,
was thin, and very soft; his body had scant hair
- perhaps he was forty, perhaps slightly older ... though,
of course, such sentimental detail is irrelevant, comrades
- it may even be in your files.... You will wish me to
proceed.... And, I shall say, in proceeding, that
Colonel Tretyakov's death was the means of prolonging
life for his brothers. Yet, at the instant, the fact of it
transfixed us. For him, he had confided, at one point,
suicide (speaking personally, you realise) was out of the
question. By the categories of our times, comrades, his
attitude might be termed superstitious - the residue,
maybe, of some childhood religion. Even so, leaving
aside the matter of his beliefs, what Officer Tretyakov
actually said was that, given a choice, he would prefer
to die against his will, however well he might resign
himself, accommodate himself, to the precise moment of
dying. And, in any case, he said, for all of us, it
would be better to die, not separately, but as it were,
collaboratively.... Can I presume, comrades, that you
have already pursued the logic of such collaboration?
And then there were two? And then there was one....
To be sure, it leaves the problem of the last man. The
last man, comrades! What of him? The question is
obvious - and I admit, it was never spoken. But our

37

entombment, I think, was hardly a theological exercise:
this is no parable I am telling. Our strategy was an
expedient, no more. Your moralist might say it sought to
postpone the ultimate problems in the hope that release
might forestall them. Myself, I would say: precisely
- that seemed the best thing to do. As it happened, of
course, our strategy collapsed long before we were
released - my brother Rubin and I, the two survivors.
And I have to confess that from the beginning, it
produced a situation none of us had properly foreseen....
In being dead, Officer Tretyakov was now utterly
separate, and the fact of his separateness was awesome,
comrades - at first, the fact, the physical separateness,
then its awesome implications.... Our brother's body
lay before us, his eyes closed - frail, I thought, so frail,
and yet ... flawless.... One minute he was asleep, the
next he was gone, and the difference was so marginal -
yet so ... awesome. All that had marked him out from us
- his face, proportions, personality - all were redundant.
What marked him out now was his lack of the one thing we
had shared throughout our entombment - the vile air we
breathed.... Comrades, consider the irony here - yes,
forgive me, another irony - I apologise - but I beg you,
consider: together we had stopped our brother's breath
- and merely for lack of that breath - for lack of our
shared, rank air, Officer Tretyakov was dead, was
different, was so awesomely separate, so still, that
his stillness, his separateness diminished his living
brothers unutterably, reduced us, dwindled us, shrank
the life within us - the life we had taken from him - shrank
that life, I say, to a despair, an emptiness so total that it
froze, it transfixed us, as we knelt about his pale body
and gazed at him - at what had been him and was now
38

nothing - only substance - inanimate, gross, separate, yet so nearly the same.... Again you doubt me, comrades! I see it! You ask: would six men who have killed a seventh for food then kneel, philosophising, while his corpse went cold among them? And I reply, in my own case, at least, it was so. I would not think to try and speak for my brothers, around me, at that moment. All I know is that we were ... entranced - and that, in our immobility, for a time, my own feelings were of despair - fear, too, I confess it - yes, fear above all, a freezing fear, a shrinking from what had to follow - and in that fear, a sense that, kneeling there, beside my brother's body, what we were about to do, the self-preservation, could not possibly be worth the shame, the abasement, it would involve. I felt diminished, I say. And you, comrades (for all my disavowals), might suggest I also felt guilt.... Guilt!... Do you know the legend of that place, the monastery of St. Peter Rabinovich - how the old, spindly monk starved himself for thirty-six days during a quarrel with some king or other, after one of the earlier wars - one of the earlier phases of the war - how he took just a cupful of water, every morning, when he woke - and how the fast then became a local tradition, with gradations of abstinence, from fourteen days for novices to the full thirty-six days, once a year, for the superiors - how the abbots were always chosen by competitive fast, and how one sixteenth-century abbot - formerly a colonel of horse - was himself so debilitated in the process that he survived barely six weeks afterwards, whereupon it was decided that future abbots should be chosen by election, with a mere token fast to follow, as proof of good heart and intention?... Having this tradition in mind,

comrades, you will wonder - won't you? - whether our
own decision to draw lots, and the resulting death of our
brother, Colonel Tretyakov, were not a little premature.
You might even suggest - mightn't you? - that the
legendary fortitude of the Rabinovich monks leads you to
suppose that we could have survived rather longer, in
the hope of rescue, before declining - albeit so
methodically - into bestiality.... Debate the question,
comrades, as you like. But forgive me if I, personally,
find it academic. My brothers and I, you will recall,
were not apprenticed in the rigours of the fast.... We
had no water! Comrades, a spoonful of water!... Nor
had our hunger a precise termination and a brimming
granary across the courtyard.... Perhaps you could
tell me, then, at what point it might have been permiss-
ible to take the course we did, remembering that our
release did not, in fact, occur until the sixtieth day - and
not forgetting your own particular eating habits and
requirements.... By the fourteenth day? The thirty-
sixth? The fortieth? Yes, comrades, perhaps the
fortieth! But Christ defeated the devil even at the
fortieth day. The forty-first, then? Or the forty-
second? And by what measure would you rule so, you
who were not present?... True, comrades, your not
being present in no way incapacitates you as judges,
since I have undertaken to provide what facts I can, as
objectively as I may, to facilitate such judgement. No,
your problem is not the facts, I imagine, it is their
interpretation. To me, the facts themselves are the
problem: to me the facts are inescapable, unexpungeable
- they appal me - doubtless they will continue to appal
me - but I have survived them - they are now part of me
- it is enough - I do not hope to exorcise them by
40

formulations of guilt - or innocence.... Of course, I am
guilty! Of what, I leave you to decide - upon the basis of
my facts. And by the facts, I say, we knelt in terror
around the pale body of Colonel Tretyakov, my brothers
and I, for some time - craven, superstitious, shamed - as
you wish.... Comrades, it was a failure of our brief
cohesion: our brother's death had made us singular
again. Though we could not yet have known it, another
pattern - of singularities - was already emerging.
Without common courage, we needed a singular courage
- and it was my brother Rubin who supplied it. From
courage, I say, not from hunger - not from desperation:
we all shared his hunger, none of us shared his courage.
For he it was who, suddenly, without warning, without a
glance at the rest of us, moved forward a little on his
knees and bent over the colonel's body and began to sway,
comrades - to sway - from side to side, rhythmically, his
head and shoulders lowering a little at each arc, until his
face was brushing the colonel's skin as he swayed - like
some ecstatic, comrades - swaying, touching the skin
- until, all at once, as we watched, he stopped, his eyes
closed, and with the slowest, calmest deliberation, he bit
into the flesh - the flesh of the right chest - and then was
still, as if in prayer, kneeling, bent - so still - for
several moments - and then raised his head and looked at
us - each of us - forced our eyes upward from the wound
- the hole he had made - from the thin trickle of blood
- and, as we watched him, he chewed and swallowed
what he had bitten and bent again, to the same place...
and one by one, we followed him - followed him, I confess
it, into a kind of delirium - and then rose, separately,
and went to our separate places on the wall, not looking
at what we had done - what we had left - and we lay,

silently.... Some of us slept, I think: all of us, at
different points, afterwards, felt the most violent inner
pains, and none of us moved, to allay them, until our
brother Rubin again moved for us - moved back across
the cell, to what we had left, and was monstrously sick
- fell to his knees and howled and howled and howled
- and for those who scrambled to help him, it was the
same. The rest of us cowered back against our walls:
I, too, comrades, I cowered into my wall - with terror.
But Officer Rubin, my brother Rubin, led us, dragged us,
to see what we had done - to go on - as we had decided
- together ... and it was the same for us: it was
unendurable - coming to that flesh once more - what
remained of it. But Rubin told us nothing had changed,
that if we drew back now, our brother Tretyakov's death
would have been wasted. Down there, on the cell floor,
he said, lay our only hope of sanity, of reason (another
paradox, comrades, another irony - wouldn't you think?)
and he forced us to our knees, to eat a second time, and
some of us followed him, some of us were revolted and
fell aside, and Officer Rubin pulled those of us back, to
eat again, while that flesh remained good - all of us
except Banishevsky, my friend Banishevsky, who would
not be moved, even by my own pleading, by the pleas of
his lifelong companion, but broke away and crawled to
his place on the wall, without a word, and covered his
ears from the sound of our feeding.... As for our
brother Rubin, comrades, he had, as it were, assumed
command - by courage, by force of character and will.
Where Colonel Tretyakov had brought us to a decision,
it was Major Rubin - a major only - Major Rubin, who
made us - at the cost, of course, of our solidarity, that
brief solidarity of equals - at the cost of some return to
42

precedence - it was Major Rubin who helped us carry
that decision through. It was Major Rubin who took
charge of the lottery; Rubin, eventually, who divided
and shared our food, who broke the bones, pulled the
limbs from their sockets, detached the heads ... the
heads of his brothers, comrades - Major Rubin detached
them and laid them together, gently, in the place where
Officer Tretyakov had been the first to die - and then
composed the ... remains - almost as if he were laying
out a uniform for inspection - carefully, meticulously....
Comrades, I cannot exaggerate my respect, my admiration,
my affection for the man. Upon himself he took the
terrible weight of our strategy - the dread, the spiritual
agony - wilfully he assumed it: having perhaps judged
some such assumption necessary, and himself, perhaps,
equipped to bear it, he took responsibility, as it were,
in a way transcending any mere matter of rank: he made
it easier for the rest of us, he softened the test of
collaboration - he helped us endure.... At what final
cost to himself, comrades, I cannot even guess. See for
yourselves there, that still model in your closed white
room, that is Officer Rubin, who is mad, you will say.
Show me your terms of reference for the word, comrades!
By my terms, it is meaningless - without application - it
touches no reality. Reality for me, comrades, is my
brother Rubin's bag of blood.... Again, be assured, I
do not seek to shock you: I merely present the facts.
And here, comrades, yes - here is a fact for your
digestion.... When a carcass is eaten, as the body of
Colonel Tretyakov was eaten - that is, forgive me, when
it is devoured - in near delirium - much blood is wasted,
that might be drunk. So when Officer Lysenko, too, was
put to death ... indeed, comrades, he was the second to

43

lose his life by a hair's breadth in our lottery ... at the
second death, I say, our brother Rubin used a piece of
the colonel's bone, delicately, to cut away a section of
poor Lysenko's skin and fold it into a little bag and drain
out his blood and bring it to us, each in turn, as we
waited, to drink, before we ate - the thick, warm blood
... and similarly when we had done - all of us except my
friend, Banishevsky, who was himself dying, secretly,
the while, behind us, at his place on the wall - dying
silently, his own blood spreading towards us, down the
shallow slope of the floor, from his corner, where he
lay, having cut his wrists - cut his wrists, comrades
- with a loose tooth, pulled from his own head.... How
casual I make that sound! A loose tooth! Pulled from
his own head! ... Comrades, it was me - kneeling beside
Lysenko's corpse - it was me who first felt Banishevsky's
blood, felt it welling against my leg, felt it spilling, cool
already, round my knee, and damming a little on
Lysenko's thigh - until suddenly I knew it should not be
there, that blood, and paddled about me, wildly, and in
a moment realised and shouted - shouted: 'Lev!'
- shouted 'Lev Alexandrovich!' and scrambled across the
cell towards him, through his blood, knowing straight
away it was too late - too late - he was dead - without a
word to anyone - to me - Vukhov - his friend - who grew
with him, in Ryazan - before the war ... and his silence,
at that instant, comrades, hurt me more than his death;
it seemed a betrayal - or rather, a rejection - is that
what I thought? - a rejection - of us all, of what we
were doing - and I beat upon him, upon my dead brother,
Banishevsky, I beat him, comrades, with my fists, as he
lay, until Rubin was beside me, as I cried, lifting me
away and feeling for a pulse, a heartbeat, and finding
44

none and saying, simply: 'He's gone. He's gone' - and I thought (this time I remember precisely) - I thought: 'It's not fair: he's got out of it again!.' - but only in the moment of shock, you understand - and even then, I knew it was wrong.... Banishevsky, comrades, was a man of distance, of reflection, and that distance took him outside our collaborate situation - he told me so. We talked continuously, he and I, in the earlier days, and he told me that, for him, our solidarity had snapped in its first expression - the destruction of Tretyakov.... For me, comrades, the first numbing sense of shame - yes, shame - I see that now - it was shame - but, for me, it did not last.... The monks of St. Peter, I presume, proved it possible to think, even to philosophise, upon an empty stomach. But on a fuller stomach, it is possible, within the hour - or less - to think quite differently. So it was with me. The new pain - of my body resuming itself - was elating, insistent: it was the pain of necessity: unconsciously - doubtless self-protectively - I found I had reaccepted the need, my body's need, for what we had done. Very quickly - like most of us, it appeared - I found my body compelling me to eat again. And the revulsion I felt at the sight of our brother Tretyakov's torn corpse was a revulsion of the body, no longer so much of the mind - a revulsion soon overridden by my body's greater need - at Officer Rubin's prompting ... and we ate again - and again - more fastidiously, more and more ... tidily - always together, always in the same place, cleaning the last bone, leaving the head and very little else - until I was amazed at the quickening of my own flesh, the renewal I felt, new blood, new cells, new life.... All real sense of identity in the colonel's flesh was gone. I found myself, almost absent-

45

mindedly, examining the organs, the intricate simplicity
of the mechanism: his body was, shall I say, objectified
- and the correctness of what we had done seemed proven
in the humming of my own body. I began to hope again,
to anticipate release.... But this time, the cycle was
shorter - the hope - the doubt - the fear and despair ....
Perhaps, comrades, that surprises you: perhaps you
would suspect that after the trauma of Colonel Tretyakov's
death, we would have managed a longer fortitude. It was
not so. We had found a means of endurance: having once
employed it, re-employment was less ... charged. I
confess: in objectifying our dead brother, I, at least,
tended more to objectify my living brothers: by another
vicious irony, our collaboration had left us the more
separate - all, I would say, now, the objects of each
other's possible survival.... But for my brother
Banishevsky, comrades, it was not the same. For the
rest of us, the odds still seemed reasonable enough, in
the circumstances - at six to one. For Banishevsky,
the whole idea of a second lottery was ludicrous,
demeaning - he told me so: he held nothing against the
rest of us, he said, we were all doing what we had to do:
but he, personally, could not come to terms with
Tretyakov's death and his own part in it: he grieved
over it, over his shame - and for him, the shame
remained. I felt renewal, he felt decay: he seemed
possessed by the thought that the colonel's body was
being transmuted within him only to exrement and urine....
Indeed, comrades! Are we all not scientists now - at
least enough to know our own insubstantiality? Render
me down, comrades, to my basic matter, and I, too,
would be left less, far less, than the size of my own
right testicle - or my left testicle (as my right testicle
46

would present itself to you): left or right, it all depends
... except to my brother, Banishevsky - for him there
were no more relativities: he said he felt himself
disembodied, that he had abandoned his own flesh, that
his mind was elevated, physically, external to his body,
somewhere high up above his head, upon the wall - and he
laughed and said perhaps the colonel's mind was up there
also - though it had not, thus far, established contact....
Having eaten once, he refused to eat again: we pleaded
with him, cajoled him, repeated all our reasoning, but
he said, simply, that, for him, it was all over - the price
was too high, the terms were no longer acceptable. For
days, he never moved: at the end, he did not even speak
- except to refuse the second lottery. Accident was one
thing, he said, wilful submission to chance was another:
he would no longer submit to anything. And by then he
was so far removed from us, his distance so great, that
not even Officer Rubin could challenge him.... But, for
all his distance, my brother Banishevsky must have
heard the death of poor Lysenko, and the preparation of
our gourd of blood - and he killed himself.... To me,
the fact of his death was a total surprise: to the others
it was obvious - Officer Rubin had no need to force him
to the lottery.... Which may raise the question in your
minds, comrades, whether Officer Lysenko need have
died at all. For my promised adherence to the facts
compels me to state he died unwillingly.... Lysenko,
comrades - a mild, slender man, once a teacher, I
believe, and short-sighted: his eyesight collapsed
almost completely in the darkness - unlike my own....
Once he told us, Banishevsky and me, that he had visited
Ryazan as a child, with his mother, a young widow,
staying with relatives, by coincidence, in the very next

47

avenue to that where his future wife, he later discovered,
was then living, as a girl, though they did not actually
meet until years afterwards, when she fell while skating
on the Neva at Leningrad and he was lucky enough to be
nearest, to help her up, and was captivated by her,
immediately, so that throughout their life together, in the
last brief peace, he had trembled whenever he looked at
her - at least he told us so.... And now I and three of
my brothers had smothered the life from this gentle man
- against his will - and our common resolve had ended,
I would term it, unhesitatingly, in murder.... Oh yes,
comrades. Surely you are not tempted to excuse me this
with some euphemism, some justification? It was murder!
Surely you are not going to say our brother Lysenko
condoned his own death, as it were, by joining the
lottery - by providing a hair from his own head for the
lottery? Comrades! These are mere niceties! I ask
you: do they apply? Be rigorous! Our entombment most
decidedly occurred: it was not, in the strict sense,
an unnatural event: it was an episode of war. And do
your legalities not extend to all episodes of the war?
Very well, then, will you tell me there are
circumstances in which murder is not a crime?... In
this instance, Officer Lysenko joined the lottery but
rejected its result, on the reasonable grounds that our
brother Banishevsky had been allowed to opt out. Why,
you may ask, did he not object before the lottery was
drawn? The answer, I suspect, lay partly in Officer
Rubin's moral command and partly in the hope, even at
odds of only five to one, of escaping selection.
Certainly these were my own thoughts at the time. As
for Officer Rubin, he explained later that he knew my
brother Banishevsky would neither wish not be able to
48

benefit from ignoring the lottery: if he remained outside
the common group, he would soon starve to death. But,
the majority having determined on the second reckoning,
it would be wrong - and dangerous - to our solidarity
- so Officer Rubin felt - to take advantage of
Banishevsky's isolation, postpone the choice and simply
wait for him to expire. And once the lottery had been
held, it would be impossible not to act upon its choice, or
else the whole strategy of the lottery would be destroyed:
therefore, Officer Lysenko, being the unfortunate one,
had to die .... By yet a further irony, of course, the
precise manner of that death destroyed the strategy in
any case. For when the choice fell upon him, Officer
Lysenko backed away, as best he could, to his place on
the wall, saying we had cheated him because he could not
see, saying for mercy's sake spare him, speaking of his
wife, his young child, railing at Banishevsky - any of us
would have done the same.... But we came upon him (he
could not see us, even then) and held him the harder as he
struggled and pressed his mouth to stop his screams and
so part throttled and part smothered him - as we had the
colonel, Tretyakov - but so differently, that having
killed poor Lysenko together, we could never trust each
other to act in common again ... except, together, to
lift Officer Lysenko's warm body from his place on the
wall to the place of the colonel's ... dismemberment
- and there, our brother Rubin, thoughtfully, began to
draw his blood, though all the while, unknown, behind us,
our silent brother Banishevsky's own blood was leaking
to waste down the faint slope of the cell floor.... Ah,
you will say, comrades, if Banishevsky had joined the
lottery, Lysenko might not have lost. Or, if
Banishevsky had killed himself an hour sooner, there

need have been no lottery, at that point, and future
lotteries might have spared Lysenko to stand here, where
I stand, now, before you.... But that is speculation,
comrades: my concern, you agree, I hope, must be with
what occurred, with the facts - and the fact is that poor
Lysenko died and I did not: my history, comrades, is
what happened. And if you persist - by your prerogative
- I can meet your questions only with more questions,
since I have no answer beyond the final answer of the
facts - as I saw them.... Why, you might say, did my
brother Banishevsky, having determined upon suicide,
not offer his death, as a sacrifice, on behalf of his
fellow sufferers? And I shall ask, in reply, by what
ordinance do you demand that a man's death shall
be as useful as his life - or rather, shall be useful in
any degree whatever? Is it a principle we have widely
honoured in this present war, or the previous - or any
other war? 'Isn't even a man's death his own?' I shall
ask. And I shall wonder at what point my brother
decided upon his death: might it not have been at the
very point, only, of Officer Lysenko's murder? Might
he not also have realised how weak he was becoming and
that before long he would lack the strength even for
suicide, but would either have to eat again or expire
through frailty? And might he not have decided upon
suicide as a gesture of the will, the disembodied mind,
in opposition to the frailty of the flesh? Self-sacrifice,
comrades - that was the response, eventually, of
Officer Blok. For Officer Banishevsky, wouldn't it
have been death on his brother prisoners' terms, not
his own? Was that why he spilled his own blood, as we
were gathering the blood of Officer Lysenko: to
register the singleness of his death - the disdain, the
50

defiance? Or was it perhaps that gouging open his
arteries was the only means of suicide he had left? And
having (if you still insist) by his defiance, permitted
Lysenko's vile killing, could he then have gone back on
his own resolve?... Believe me, comrades, I cannot
tell - for, in his last days, I, his childhood friend, knew
Officer Banishevsky less than the others knew him, and
the others knew him hardly at all. Perhaps, again, you
will accept, therefore, that I should simply present the
facts - as I recall them: and the salient fact here is that
suddenly there were only four of us alive. Our contract,
now, was irreparably broken: little as we may have
realised it, at that terrible moment, we were already
deep in the logic of personal response. Short of release,
the final pattern of our torment was fixed to the exclusion
of chance.... For the time being, however, our brother
Rubin's command remained: in fact these, I would say,
were the days of his most complete dominance, his total
care and control of our mutual situation - for the benefit
of all ... that is, all four surviving.... He it was, as
we knelt, at that same spot, in that same ritual, who
divided our sustenance between us, taking account of our
experience to apportion the ... pleasanter parts as
fairly as could be managed - if anything, denying himself
the delicacies.... Oh yes, comrades, delicacies! A
relative term, you understand.... As for me, the
distress of my friend's death was desolating. Maybe a
full day I stayed at the wall, without a word from Rubin
except words of comfort and concern - and then, as he
expected, I took food again. Only a day after my
brother Banishevsky's suicide, I was eating his flesh,
with as little scruple, comrades, and as discriminately,
as fastidiously as I had finally helped devour the colonel

51

himself.... Forgive me, I say this not to shock, not in
remorse, but as an undeniable fact. Mentally,
emotionally, I had made the necessary ... adjustment:
physically, we all - all four remaining - soon had
sharpened bones to eat with, while our brother Rubin
was quickly developing the most remarkable surgical
skill.... But our adjustments were divisive: well as
we fed, we rarely spoke now: even Rubin - the
encouraging Rubin - gradually began to turn inward upon
himself. For this time, even with two bodies to feed on,
the period of safety, of respite, was still shorter: the
cycle of hope, the expectation of release, the certainty
of a new offensive, of the monastery's recapture, even of
the enemy's return - this time these fantasies were yet
briefer and the subsequent despair yet more profound
- and profounder for the suspicison with which we now
viewed each other, since, after the death of our brother
Lysenko, a further lottery was out of the question - we
knew that - and none of us knew, but each of us
wondered, what the next mode of decision might be ... all
of which, slowly, sapped Officer Rubin's authority and
plunged him into ever deeper quietness and gloom.... In
the event, the confrontation of the final four (for such it
had become) was resolved by Officer Blok, who chose
- as I said - the gesture of self-sacrifice.... Blok, who
had latterly begun to pray, with increasing fervency, in a
kind of rapture, broken by repeated assurances that his
prayers encompassed us all.... Comrades, Officer Blok
seemed to draw much comfort from the legend of St. Peter,
the legend of the monastery itself, the tradition of self-
denial. And suddenly - it was on the morning of the
fortieth day - by my counting - on that morning, our
brother Blok made what amounted to an announcement
52

- in the circumstances - saying that he, personally, had at last concluded our position was hopeless, that we could expect no reprieve, that he could no longer see any agreed way of retaining our dignity (as he put it), that we were again almost afraid to sleep for fear of each other, that a pact, a collective suicide was impossible, because we now lacked the collective trust for such a step and because, in any case, he, personally, would never contemplate taking his own life, but that some initiative (in his own rather formal phrase), some personal initiative was required, since, he felt, we had lost the will to endure, we had severally contracted a weakness of will that pandered to the quickening weakness of our bodies, as if we had all, unconsciously, begun to desire an end, a termination, and therefore he proposed, if we would agree, that he should accept, himself, what the lottery had brought to Tretyakov and Lysenko, that he should lay down his life (as he put it), to reduce our dilemma, for he, at least, he said, could now cheerfully do so in the reasonable hope of salvation thereafter, a hope which, though he recognised its risk of delusion, though he accepted its wilfulness, was nonetheless real to him, at that moment, despite all he had undergone, and thus he would ask that we permit him the solace of final prayer, for us as much as for himself, and then do with him as we would, thereby allowing what he frankly admitted was his release from a trial that had become intolerable.... It was, I think, an extraordinary statement, especially from one who had, at first, shown such patience, such stubborn humour - from one whose songs and peasant stories had brought us merciful diversion in the early days of our entombment.... But now, comrades, in reply to his proposition, no one said

53

a word, not Rubin, not I, not Officer Lubianko - in fact, our brother Lubianko had not once spoken for something above a week.... Rubin never even looked up: he was gazing, incessantly, at his own wrist, under the effect, it seemed, of some deep change, some metamorphosis.... Taking our silence as consent, I must suppose, Officer Blok knelt, indeed, to pray, and stayed kneeling a good hour, I would guess - utterly still and silent - then rose, blessed us, hoped salvation for us, if not on earth then elsewhere, wished us good-bye, kissed us, each, at our places on the wall, then lay down and fell into some sort of trance - at least I now take it to have been so.... None of us moved to him: none of us moved at all. Frankly, for some inexplicable reason, we ignored him. And by the next day, when I myself finally stirred, to wake him, he was dead. His eyes were closed, his face expressionless, his beard hiding all trace of the weeks before - his death, again, an astonishment.... Remembering, now, I can see how wasted Officer Blok had become: as I said, he was always the slightest of us - the apex of our pyramid, you will recall - but now he was withered, the bones shone white through his remaining flesh, they jutted, protruded - you will have seen the like.... I remember how disinterestedly I had watched him at his prayers: I remember the self-possession with which he merely lay down, full length, to die.... Do you doubt me, comrades? Very well, you are correct. What I rashly assume to have been Blok's self-possession may well have been exhaustion - the concentration, perhaps, of a man at the last of his strength and mustering that strength for some final gesture.... But forgive me, I cannot think so: I cannot think Officer Blok was indeed exhausted. Very near

54

it, to be sure - but if his strength was spent, from where did he summon the animation, the business-like animation, of his speech (I can only term it a speech) of the previous day? For I do not recall that speech as one of fatigue, rather one of decision.... Not that it matters, of course, for the purpose of presenting the facts. Decision or fatigue? At this distance, in this room, it can only be a question of interpretation, not of fact. And the fact is that on the fortieth day of our entombment, Officer Blok laid down and died... and no one noticed.... That, too, comrades, that was a fact. I must confess: I observed the death of Officer Blok: I watched it, from an icy unconcern, as if it were a demonstration on some doctor's table.... How, then, can I properly report it? My duty, I have said, is to the facts. But I also have a duty to my brothers in this case - and to none of them, necessarily, would the facts have seemed the same.... At the last, did Officer Blok abdicate his life or did he simply die?... There is the world of difference, comrades. And it does matter: it matters if I am to keep faith with Captain Blok. I know that now.... Comrades, Blok declared a readiness to die; he lay down, evidently expecting to die; and he died.... That is what I saw. Does it answer the question? I think not. But I can hardly tell you what I did not see.... I did not see, did not register, the precise moment of Officer Blok's death - my inwardness prevented it.... Do I misrepresent him, then? The problem troubles me.... Similarly, comrades, my witness of my friend Banishevsky's suicide: can it be wholly reliable - is it wholly to be trusted? I ask myself: have I done him less than justice? For the act of suicide is not widely approved, even (or perhaps especially) in the theatre of war.... But Vukhov,

you might say - Vukhov, look here, you promised us only
your report: it is up to us, your judges, to do justice
- you stick to the facts. And I thank you, comrades, for
your understanding. But I would say, further: consider
the difficulties of the facts - how problematic they are,
how the very act of description can distort them. Take
my brother Lysenko's death: did my description of it
leave a certain hint of cowardice on his part? If so, I
beg you, comrades, dismiss it! My brother Lysenko's
reaction to the lottery was one of anger, of helplessness,
a sense of having been duped, made scapegoat.... Or
was it? How can I tell? And how may I describe the
final death - the death of Officer Lubianko - without
doing some disservice - at least by your legalities - to my
dear brother Rubin?... It is complex, comrades, this
business of the facts - their iron malleability....
Perhaps, for a moment, I might speak of myself - it is
easier.... You may still wonder (frankly, I, too, have
begun to wonder) what it was that enabled me to survive
our shared imprisonment when five of my brothers died
- and to survive it so differently from Officer Rubin....
For one thing, to be sure, I was fortunate: I escaped
the lottery. Again, perhaps, my body must have proved
... reliable - my mind, or, if you prefer, my spirit,
satisfactorily adaptable. Also, it is possible, for me,
circumstances, and my own moods, never reached the
precise confluence that prompted some singular decision
- as, for instance, with Officer Blok and my brother
Banishevsky. My own response was merely to try and go
on: but not, I think, from any particular strength of will
- rather for lack, as I saw it, of any better alternative
.... Believe me, I say this not in any spirit of abjection
or formal self-criticism: I genuinely wonder, as I make

56

my report, whether an important element in my continuance might not have been a swathing apathy of the spirit - a spiritual malnutrition.... You will recognise the paradox, of course - yet another paradox ... an apathy that carries it s own habitual economy, its instinctive conservation. For I see, now, comrades: generally, I found myself doing only what was required, taking no initiative (except in the matter of the time), expending little, responding to circumstance, never dictating to it.... Was it, then, by my pliancy, my very ordinariness, that I survived?... This may not redound much to my credit as an officer, but I must, in all honesty, ask myself: what was my basic response to our entombment? Was it only from the pale centre of the spectrum that I drew my courage?... Courage! Comrades, I use the word ironically: call it what you will - I prefer stubbornness - or, more candidly, inertness.... The term, of course, is relative. It may be that I simply struggled less than my brothers. Yes, could that be it? That I fought less - either for or against certain responses? If so, I would not count it a weakness, any more than I would count my survival a strength - only a difference. And I feel neither remorse nor pride in such difference - neither remorse that I depended, at a certain point, on my brother Rubin's costly struggle to sustain me: nor pride that, in the end, my brother Rubin was, to some extent, sustained by me. It matters, I say: the difference always matters. But comrades, can it reasonably affect your estimation of my fitness for return to the war?... Despite our difference, Rubin and I would both have died eventually, had not Officer Scriabin freed us. And if Scriabin had not freed us - or freed us later - my courage would have been put to the test of some

decision: at the last confrontation, with my brother
Rubin, I, too, would have been compelled to some
singularity or other. Had it happened so and had I still
survived, doubtless I, too, would have viewed our facts
differently - more in the light, perhaps, of that
decision, than of my previous acquiescence. I would not
have been the same man.... But then, in truth,
comrades, I cannot fully recognise even the man I have
just presented to you: that inertness, that acquiescence,
how does it relate to the flux of my moods, my cell-
moods? Comrades, are not all such terms of self-
description unreliable? I was mistaken to toy with them
.... And yet, perhaps it is not entirely uninstructive
- the way, even here, before you, the line of my defence
was turned, despite myself - by the sense, my sudden
sense of the invisibility of poor Blok's death. How
sentimental that makes me! As if it mattered, at that
point, to Officer Blok, whether his death was noted or
ignored: whether I, personally - or you, comrades
- should judge it a death by exhaustion or a death by
resolve! Without proper information, I regret, the
question must be speculative. And speculation, I think,
is not rewarding - tempting, yes, but unreliable - so
much the prey of interest and mood.... Now I generalise
again! Do you see, comrades, why I have preferred to
rely, despite their dangers, on the facts - as I saw - and
recall them. For I am something of an expert in the play
of moods - prison-moods, I say, that might hold, like fog,
for days, or switch and change, by the hour, by the
minute even, dependent on factors of fatigue, digestion,
sexuality.... To be sure, comrades - sexuality! It
proved, in the circumstances, a factor of remarkable
resilience - a factor we all seven had to cope with - and
58

coped in our several ways, some more, some less ...
successfully - nonetheless, a critical factor (though less
so at the very beginning and the end) in the play of moods
- and that play, so unpredictable, so various, so hard,
at times, to fix - for safety.... For my own part,
however, comrades, I can say that certain habits, if you
prefer, certain disciplines of mind, certain routines,
were a help. Like the time, comrades - the time - such a
simple thing - yet for me it became, shall I say, a
pendulum - a slow metronome to the flux of my emotions
.... Often, it seemed we were the earth's last creatures:
I lost all apprehension of the world outside our four close
walls. The universe shrunk to a narrow cell! It is a
cliche of sorts, I know - like its complement, the dream
of boundlessness - the deliberate reverie that melts the
walls and draws up the world again from the sediment of
each separate life, conjuring the private stock of images,
memories, selecting from them, repeating, practising,
adjusting them to a comforting script ... my wife, always
my wife, the children, my politic sister.... But for me,
comrades, there was always the time, too - to break the
dream ... the light, entering our cell each morning,
through the little grille, high on the wall - entering,
extending, pausing, retracting - the pendulum of light,
the faultless metronome that established and re-
established our reality and therefore limited my moods
.... In the first weeks, we had, as it were, compared
notes on the calendar. But even before Colonel
Tretyakov's death, some of my brothers had grown
irritated with the procedure. Eventually, I took to
making a mark, for each day, upon my wall - with a piece
of bone. Soon, this, also, became an irritation - the
scratching of the bone, the ranks of the days, mounting in

59

their sevens. After an interval, I began making my marks
whenever the others were asleep, which was not often,
for, in that respect, we had become disorientated - we
slept irregularly, if at all. Patiently, I saved up my days
for the moment when I might bring the wall-calendar up to
date - graving the marks with care - clean, white, in the
wall-stone - and every now and again going back to the
start, to elongate them. It was an obsession of sorts
- like our secret fears, our secret calculations.
Perhaps the others noticed: if so, they said nothing,
made no further objection: the calendar had finally
become my private game - and we all, I assure you,
comrades, had our private games.... But in the last
days before Officer Blok's death, my calendar itself
broke down. We were consumed, the remaining brothers,
in a terrible lethargy - at least, that is how I would
characterise it now, my own condition: a sullen waiting
- for the next crisis.... The killing of Lysenko had
destroyed our strategy, I say: we had lost control: a
pyramid of four would not even reach the window! All of
us, I think, could feel the boil of our tension rising:
collectively, there was nothing more we could do - or
wanted to do - except wait for it to burst.... And there
was Banishevsky's suicide: it must have affected me,
personally, more than I knew. Or am I guessing?
Comrades, I cannot be sure: I am at a loss to explain it,
that dreadful, hostile torpor. All I know is that I woke on
the forty-first morning to see Officer Blok lying, full
length, in the centre of the cell, as he had been when I
fell asleep - and for some hours before. I remembered
his declaration: though I had ignored it, I found I
remembered every word, and suddenly I felt it wrong
that he had delivered up his life to us and that we, in our
60

despair, had rejected him - and here he was, still lying there.... I crawled across from my place on the wall. I was going to say: 'Forgive us, Yuri' - Yuri was his Christian name - Yuri Nikolayevich - I was going to say: 'Forgive us, Yuri, we cannot do it' - or something like that - some such formula, some excuse or other - something similarly unsatisfactory - but when I came to him I could see he was dead: he was cold - a mere corpse - shrivelled - his poor body witness to what he had suffered.... I sat and looked at him, at the manner of his going, and I think (by another paradox, comrades) that his going returned me to myself, drew me back from the dark, sullen fathoms of my dread, my grief.... Once more, comrades, consider the irony - how my brother Blok, having reached his own decision - having offered himself for sacrifice on our behalf - how he then died in the most commonplace way - of some more natural cause - how he died untended, ignored, and then, how his thin corpse, flat, straight, the hands crossed at the breast - how his corpse - not the gesture of his dying - slowly restored me, at least, to myself, as I gazed at it, as I understood how far I had sunk from myself, that I had rejected his death - and yet, strangely, how every instant of our waking life in the cell during those two lost days was printed on my mind, like the negative of a photograph, I would say, and that as I sat, in the dawn of the forty-first day, silently, surveying Officer Blok's body, the stupor lifted - or rather, it dissolved - and I felt amazingly clear-headed, clear-minded - able to continue, to go on.... Blok's quiet wasting, his struggle to resolve himself, I had seen it all, comrades, but the knowing of what I had seen, the understanding, had been delayed - by a despair which I would properly term a

lethargy of sensibility. Now, too, I saw my brother
Rubin's own inwardness, the cowl of it, the growth of it,
as the meaning of his assumed role was destroyed. I saw
Officer Lubianko sickening: I saw how quickly the sickness was beginning to take him - a sickness of the
stomach, which ground him woefully; a failure of the
chest, which made him cough almost incessantly - a cough
which had been worsening for some time, which had
doubtless contributed to our depression, but a cough
which I seemed never to have actually heard until then,
sitting there, beside my brother Blok's body.... And the
light - I saw the light, comrades, the lost days, shrunk,
perfectly, to scale, as I sat, and I knew there were two
days to make up on the calendar, two days, most exactly,
and a third, now, for the sun was entering our cell once
more, through the tiny grille, high on the outer wall
- entering, lengthening, fixing, retracting - to mark a
further day - and the slow pendulum moved again, in its
proportion, for me, and when Rubin, also, stirred, and
saw me, sitting, beside Blok's corpse, and crawled
across, from his place on the wall, I was able to say:
'I'm afraid he's gone' - just so - so precisely.... But
Rubin said nothing, made no reaction. Almost without
pause - like a man in a dream, I thought - he pulled
Officer Blok's light body, by the armpits, to the place,
the same place where Colonel Tretyakov had died, then
went to fetch his collection of sharpened bones, from his
own place, on the wall, and began his careful surgery,
first, again, stripping a patch of skin to hold the draining
blood - while I moved to Lubianko - coughing - and woke
him and tried to tell him ... but when Rubin brought the
gourd, to drink, Lubianko, raised on one elbow, dashed it
aside so that it spilt, partly on the floor, partly upon
62

himself, on his legs, so that he twisted to his knees and tried to wipe himself clean, with his hands, wiping his hands on the floor, only there was more blood on the floor, and as he struggled to clean himself, he knelt in it and cried out, with such disgust, such revulsion, and scrambled back along the wall, to a new place, coughing violently, bent upon himself, trying to raise saliva from his dry mouth to spit on his legs, his knees, the hair of his groin, to clean himself, and the spit, such as he could summon, mixing with the phlegm of his coughing, on his hands, and the blood, too, now, on his hands, and all the wetness rubbing to a paste on his hands, until he forgot the rest of himself and fell into a coil, on the floor, at his new place, in an agony of coughing, his rubbing, scraping hands plunged down into his stomach and his body curled round them, shuddering, his head almost between his knees.... Rubin, restored, I thought, in the emergency, knelt down to help - and I with him - to comfort. But for Lubianko, there was no help, no comfort: at the touch of our hands, comrades, he squirmed away from us, until Rubin rose, knowing - as he had known with my friend Banishevsky - that there was nothing to be done, and he picked up the patch of skin from the floor, and we returned, he and I, to the corpse of our dead brother, Blok.... Later, considerably later, when his pain receded, his coughing subsided, Lubianko asked for food - and Rubin took him food - but each time, within minutes, he had vomited it back. Then he would weep, poor man, in terror, saying his body was rejecting what he had done, that his dead brothers were destroying him - from within. Or he would accuse us, Rubin and me, of poisoning him, saying that we fed him the rotten flesh, the parts that would sicken him, because

he was too ill to fend for himself. And he would refuse
more food, would scream if we ventured anywhere near
- to help him ... until the hunger became too great again
and he would eat and vomit and fall back into his fever of
pain.... It was appalling to have to watch him suffer - to
watch so uselessly. Yet at his first fit, when our brother
Blok's blood spilt upon him, Rubin and I had decided,
unspokenly, that Officer Lubianko would be the next to
die - not, comrades, as a matter of selfish calculation
but as a matter of fact - a fact that needed no calculation
but was evident in Lubianko's worsening illness....
Effectively, he would select himself for the next death
- by dying. No need of a strategy: that was clear - on
the instant - both to Rubin and myself: no need for a
decision of any kind, save the decision of our brother
Lubianko's body - and no matter how well we might tend
him, that decision would not be altered. The astonishing
thing was that we had not seen all this before; that, in
our sullen isolation, we had somehow failed to
appreciate how ill Lubianko had become. Even Blok had
not known it, as he struggled towards his own resolution.
And if he had known it, you might ask, would he still
have offered up his life - and died?... If, comrades! If
only! If only the war had not been so cruel, if Officer
Blok had been an infantryman or an admiral of the fleet, if
he had been born across the frontier, or been born with
some disablement or not been born at all.... Forgive me:
the fact of the matter is merely that, for some reason, the
degree of Lubianko's pain escaped us. In part, I suspect,
this was because the man was so big: it seemed
unthinkable his great body should fail. For Officer
Lubianko was magnificent, comrades - deep-chested, with
enormous shoulders and rich black hair. In the early
64

days he had entertained us by rippling his muscles to our
songs. His thighbone, comrades, this - my silent witness,
you remember - this was his thighbone. Even his penis
was extraordinary.... Comrades, please, I beg you, do
not understand me coarsely.... Let me tell you that
Lubianko's penis was a most superb and capable
instrument and that his stories of its repeated and
glorious use, in his harvest time, outdid the rival stories
of all his brothers - my own included - in the moments of
ribaldry - before the colonel's death.... Oh come now,
comrades, we were only men, imprisoned there together!
Do I make any other claim for us? And what men, I
wonder, cast naked into one cell, could quite resist the
trivialities of comparative anatomy?... Again I
generalise, in my very question. Excuse me, comrades.
But believe me, too - that I speak of Lubianko's prowess
with affection - because, in truth, I would not have the
story of his agonies demean him in your eyes.... I
repeat: I would hope to say nothing (as I recognise
nothing) that might in any way slander my companions.
And I stress this not only from consideration for their
families, their ... reputations, but also from
consideration of the facts. I must speak carefully, yet,
with the greatest care, I cannot avoid saying that my
brother Lubianko suffered woefully before his death: in
view of the manner of his dying, I cannot pretend otherwise - and pain such as his, despair such as his, are not,
I suggest, always conducive to dignity. That is why I
speak now of Officer Lubianko as I knew him before his
sickness - a powerful man, a man most inordinately proud
of the daintiness of his wife - such a tiny girl, he would
say, and him so grand and so gentle with her, that she
called him her sun, he said, her rising sun.... And this

man it was, comrades, whose body wilted most, I think, in our entombment.... Looking back, of course, I can see the signs, the clues to his collapse. For instance, the cold: Lubianko was the most affected of us by the cold - the night chill.... Even at the end - high summer outside the cell - the dark hours were often miserably cold - without clothes, often without sleep, alone, on the stone floor. So, in the first days, the May days, you can imagine, comrades, how we huddled together, at night, shivering, for warmth: how Rubin, the gymnast, led us in exercises, twice, often three times a day - at the véry beginning - press-ups, handstands, yes, and leap-frog - all with a determined jollity - to keep up morale, as he put it - and to combat the cramps, the pains of chilled nakedness.... But even after we had retreated to our walls, our separateness, even after the colonel's death, Lubianko - his whole body quivering convulsively - would still edge, silently, imploring, across to Lysenko, who lay nearest him, and curl himself around the hoop of Lysenko's own chill form and try to sleep there.... Then, when Lysenko, too, was gone - so violently - even that comfort was denied him, and Lubianko spent hours at a time, clenched rigid, his teeth chattering as he struggled to still his shivering. The one time he escaped the cold was, finally, when the fevers took him and he would burn as badly as he had shivered only moments before.... How ironic, comrades - to be eaten, inwardly, devoured, I say, by a sickness he could never beat out, no matter how he clutched and clawed at it, no matter how he wriggled, how he twisted - no escaping the tiny pit of his own destruction....
From the forty-fifth day, by my reckoning, Lubianko did not even try to eat - he simply screamed - hour by hour

by hour - no begging now, no cursing, no complaining,
just that scream, constantly - broken only by the faints,
the brief sleeps of exhaustion.... Sometimes he would
get to his knees, his hair dripping with sweat, his face
caked in his own foaming, and he would crawl out from
his wall towards us, blinded by his fever, calling for us
- where were we, why wouldn't we help him? - and then
roll backwards on to his haunches and slowly totter over,
already unconscious, on to his side, and would wake
again, as we moved him, and wriggle free of us as we
brought him to his wall, and scream again, and scream
.... It was appalling, I say. Yet soon - I confess it -
my mind was closed to that screaming, closed to
Lubianko's agony. There was nothing to be done for him:
he would accept nothing from us - even to be touched
compounded his pain. And to listen to it, helplessly, was
unendurable. Comrades, to be outside all that torment,
yet to be assaulted by it - the appalling sound of it
- inescapable, irrepressible ... it was hateful: Lubianko
became hateful - I admit it - I began to hate him for his
agony - the discomfort it brought me. Therefore I
stopped listening - as simply as that. Not deliberately,
not by an act of will or concentration - not by displacing
the screams with some remembered problem of
engineering: I merely stopped listening. I remained
aware of Lubianko's suffering - the stages of his crisis:
had he called for help I would have heard, I know it. But
of his crying I heard only an echo, as it were - because to
go on hearing more would have been insupportable.... It
was not, I think, an unprecedented reaction - if not,
perhaps, entirely praiseworthy.... My brother, Rubin,
however, seemed to hear everything: every modulation
of Lubianko's pain seemed etched upon him, physically.

67

Lying there, on his side, his head cradled on his arm,
unmoving, as if hypnotised, he watched, watched it all,
heard it all, avoided nothing - the forty-seventh day -
the forty-eighth - until, on the forty-ninth day, by my own
reckoning, I suddenly noticed he had begun to scratch his
neck, rhythmically, as he lay, from just below the ear.
Twice, three times, I moved across to stop him; straight
away, he started again, until the fourth time, I lifted him,
and left him sitting with his shoulders to the wall.
Finally, on the fiftieth day, he began to rock backwards
and forwards, rather as he had swayed (you may remember) over Colonel Tretyakov's body. Then all at once,
as if some guyrope had snapped, he was on his feet,
half-standing, bent, and bounding over the cell to where
Lubianko lay, screaming - and in a moment he had
strangled him - only a moment, comrades, and Rubin had
broken Lubianko's neck - I heard the sound, I heard it
distinctly - the crack of Lubianko's neck breaking in
Rubin's great hands - those hands ... all his pity, all his
pent emotion hardened those hands, I would say, as they
seized Lubianko by the throat and put him to death - to
sleep ... It was done so quickly, so powerfully - I think
Lubianko cannot have suffered, cannot even have realised
what was happening: there was no sound, no real struggle
only a start of horror in his face - a sightless, contorted
panic - and then he was dead.... Rubin never looked at
him: he just knelt, and stayed kneeling, with Lubianko's
body twisted sideways before him, his hands set fast,
locked, rigid, round the throat, and he, gazing,
expressionless, somewhere towards the cell door....
For myself, I felt only relief - relief at the silence - at
an end to all that pain. Nothing more. Only relief....
Standing here, before you, comrades, it would be easy
68

to pretend otherwise, claiming to have felt the most
moving pity for the last of my dead brothers. But it
would be a charade. My pity for Lubianko, my
compassion, were overwhelmed by the weight of his pain
and my own helplessness before it. Since I could not
soften that pain, I retreated from it, instinctively: I
suppose I withdrew my compassion - to save myself
being crushed. Lubianko's screams were like needles
in my brain. I fled from them, into a kind of alert
neutrality - I confess it - without shame, comrades - I
confess it as a fact - that is what happened - I see it
clearly - I was an observer, too, at Lubianko's death.
And my brother Rubin, who could not escape the
piercing needles, who could not - or perhaps would not
- hide from those screams - he was the actor in that
death - as I expected.... Yes, comrades, I knew what
Officer Rubin would do - a man of his courage, his
understanding, his resolve. At least, to be more
accurate, I was not surprised - simply shocked, in the
physical sense, startled - at the suddenness, the force,
the merciful force of what he did.... And was that all?
you will ask. Was that my only reaction - to be
'startled' - merely 'startled' - when poor, sick, defenceless Lubianko was strangled before my eyes? Of course
you ask it, comrades! What was this neutrality of mine,
you ask, this preservative neutrality, that let me watch
unmoved (as it must seem) the murder of a man whose
long torment I had shared, whose agony I had witnessed?
... Oh comrades, your categories again! Murder, you
say - we must say 'murder', mustn't we? Very well, then.
Was it murder for Officer Rubin to put a term to such
suffering? Was it murder or was it mercy? Ah, you will
say, did Officer Lubianko ask to die, did he ever beg to

69

be released his pain? And I must answer 'No': he never even spoke of death: he merely suffered - and screamed - interminably - day after day. So forgive me, comrades, if I, myself, ask a question - on my brother Rubin's behalf, as it were.... What class, what category would you invoke to cover the act of inactivity in such a case - the act of doing nothing?... But you sense the trap, don't you? And you say: who is to tell how serious Lubianko's ailment was? Degrees of pain are not always a reliable guide to the likelihood of mortality: had we been freed at that fiftieth day, might not Lubianko have survived?... Being no physician, comrades, how can I reply - except to suggest, once more, that such retro-spection must be academic? I repeat: we were not released until the sixtieth day. Are you, sitting here, prepared to say how long Officer Rubin, lying there, should have watched our brother Lubianko squirm and listen to him scream? Or do you, perhaps, question the motive of this murder? Is that it, comrades? Do you suspect that Lubianko was strangled, not for mercy but for food?... Please, I beg you, do not be afraid of your own questions. Are you not the judges in this matter? Let me admit: the question is quite reasonable: neither Rubin nor myself had ... eaten - for some little time previously.... But the facts, I think (as I recall them), will provide your answer. For I myself watched my brother Rubin burst - burst, comrades - under the mounting pressure of Lubianko's agony. I saw him absorb his brother's pain - lying exposed, unprotected, he endured it, wilfully, without reaction, without expression, his eyes, it seemed, as flat as mirrors - he let the pulse of Lubianko's pain irradiate him - and at last, when the pressure was no more to be endured, he stopped it - as if
70

he knew, by that proxy torment, the limit of Lubianko's
endurance, too, had come.... But the speed, comrades,
the strength, the control with which he moved! Suddenly
he ceased rocking and sat, where I had leaned him,
against the wall, summoning himself, I would say - having
decided it must be done, deciding how it must be done -
then, having done it - quicker and with less hurt,
perhaps, than any doctor's morphia - having done it, I
say, he knelt, locked in the completion of it, until I
moved to him again and tried to bring him away. But he
only went back to his wall - for his collection of bones
- and then returned and, without once looking at
Lubianko's contorted face, he severed the head, at the
neck, and placed Lubianko's head at the end of the row of
heads - the fifth head - and dragged the torso to the
place of the - remains ... only this time he left the body
untouched and instead went, silently, to his own place on
the wall and lay down again, fingering his throat, his
hands bloody to the wrists.... Ask yourselves,
comrades, was that a murder? And since, by your
categories, you must say it was, ask yourselves, I beg
you: wasn't that murder an act of love, an act of
courage and compassion?... Thank you, comrades - I
thank you: in your pity, you agree - you excuse - or
should I say absolve? - very well, you absolve my
brother Rubin (insofar as it is in your power) of his
technical offence - as offence it was - within your
categories.... But your absolution - I sense it - is
withheld from me: you are disturbed still, that I
watched as Lubianko suffered - as he died - and that I
did nothing. May I ask, then, where, precisely, was
my inactivity an offence? Was I at fault, as it were, not
to join in Lubianko's murder - or in failing to prevent

it?... Again, of course, the judgement must be yours, comrades. For me, the problem did not arise - at least, not as so exact a paradox. I state it now only in appreciation of your dilemma - or what I take to be your dilemma: I state it as a reasonable response to my description of Lubianko's death. But forgive me, the response is also an external one, just as your judgement is external. Please, do not misunderstand: I recognise the response as I submit willingly to the judgement: for satisfactory administration of the war, clearly, there must be such judgements. But upon what basis will you judge me? My defence rests entire upon that question: in other words, it rests confidently upon the facts - as I recall them. For ironically, at the level of recall, my facts are simpler than their interpretation. Indeed, it strikes me that, in these proceedings, I have much the easier part ... I apologise! I attempt no evasion. But if I were here to judge, whom could I reasonably judge except myself? And what tribunal would accept a man's self-estimate as testimony? Me, my own character witness! It would be against the rules, comrades, wouldn't it?... Of course, as judges, you will draw conclusions about my character, my nature, from my presentation of the facts - according to the rules. No matter that my facts are my defence - that my nature shapes their presentation, consciously shapes them, confessedly shapes them, to procure my readmission to the war - shapes them, therefore, as witness to my character - which self-witness is beyond the rules.... Comrades, once more I ask your patience. I merely wish to establish that I make no pretence, practise no subterfuge - I need none. I do not shirk self-judgement: there, too, I accept my responsibility. Yet I hope I do not brandish it. Which of us ever truly sits in judgement on himself? How is it possible to judge so, objectively? And if I judge myself other than objectively, don't I judge only by the categories distilled from my nature, my own experience, making guilt and innocence alike the most trivial formulae, secretions, in a sense, of childhood? And what then of sentencing - and punishment - of clemency - and reprieve? Judging myself, I think, might be more wisely termed knowing myself: it is more accurate, don't you agree? Self-knowledge? My testimony before you is shaped by what I know (or think I know) of myself: it includes, if you like, my own judgement of myself - incorporates it, as a matter of course. What I know of myself - my conscience, as it were - is implicit in the manner, the form, the very intent of my defence. And since explicit self-judgement is not allowed, I suggest you can ask no more of me. I am, if you wish, my own facts, my own defence: I present myself, without dissimulation, for your judgement.... To be sure, such judgement may turn upon estimates of my nature different from my own - upon a measure broader, or more severe, than my self-knowledge - upon an unrecognised layer of myself betrayed, or rather, uncovered, by my facts, my presentation of the case. If that be so, so let it be: I cannot tell what I do not know. I simply offer my report, together with what sense of my nature it reveals. And my report, comrades, is almost complete: that is to say, my report of our imprisonment to the point of our release, my brother Rubin and me. Should you still wish to speculate upon what might have happened had we not been released, that, again, is your prerogative ... but only, I suggest, as my brothers, not as my judges in deliberation. The facts, I agree, provide

73

some basis for surmise. But no more. And surmise, I submit, is not a matter for this hearing.... Comrades, forgive me! Can I seriously expect you to separate your personal from your judicial selves? Are you not my fellow combatants, even as my judges, and can such shared commitment ever quite be banished from your judging? I see it now: there is no difference: any surmise upon the course of that final confrontation - between Officer Rubin and myself - had we not been freed in time to avert it - any such surmise will depend upon your assessment of my facts - your judgement of my state of mind - my brother Rubin's state of mind. The judgement bears the surmise - and since I cannot avoid your judgement, how can I hope to avoid your surmise?... But equally, comrades, I feel I cannot be expected to assist these divinations. I can only say, as I have already said, that I do not know what I would have done - at the sixty-first day - or the sixty-fifth - or the seventieth. It never came to that. All I have left to give you, therefore, are the remaining facts (few as they seem) from the death of Lubianko to the point of our release, ten days later.... You will notice, comrades, how precise I am, once more, about the time. Yet I have to acknowledge that, at the last, my calendar lied. From day fifty-four, I no longer scratched the marks: I kept the days but did not mark them. I kept my fingernails, too - pared and bit and scraped them neat: there was nothing to be done about my hair and beard, even my body, but now I kept my fingernails. And similarly, I kept the days - counting at the moment the sunlight touched the wall above my head - but I did not mark them ... out of resignation, perhaps. I still resisted, but I would say I was melting into a calm of resignation....
74

And then there was my brother Rubin: after the fifty-fourth day, even the least sound - the sound of my scratching on the wall - would wake and frighten him.... That morning a bird flew in through the little grille - a small bird - maybe a sparrow - out of the light, into the dark - flying round high up under the roof, with nowhere to settle, looping lower now and again, the flapping of its wings like the flap of great, fast sails in the silence .... While we had been alone, neither Rubin nor I had moved: Lubianko's body was untouched ... I remember, it was very cold, even at midday ... Rubin lay along his wall, face to the stone. I sat at my place, in total calm. Comrades, I have never felt so relaxed: it was as if my body had slowed, and slowed, almost to zero. I hardly slept in the full three days: I was beyond sleep - beyond hope, beyond despair, beyond hunger, it seemed, beyond thirst, beyond pain. There was nothing to do but wait. No need yet of a further initiative. So I waited, at rest, at ease, knowing I had nothing to fear from my brother Rubin, in his rigid separateness - knowing instinctively that the next stage was up to me, that by default, as it were - by Rubin's spiritual exhaustion - the initiative would now be mine - eventually ... and the care.... Perhaps you are sceptical of such calm, comrades, such stillness, at that stage in our torment - but I assure you, it was so - until, on the morning of the fifty-fourth day, the bird flew into our cell, without even touching the window bars, and could find nowhere to settle, and needing it, could find no way out, from the darkness to the light, but struck against the bars now, flapping, flapping, striking the bars, striking, falling down their length, then retreating a little, rising again and still, in its panic, unable to get through, and falling and retreating.... To me, comrades, the bird was a matter of indifference - an error - a chance intrusion - certainly not a consolation - hardly even a reminder - only a bird. Either it would escape or it would not: neither way would if affect the pattern of our suffering.... But I was wrong, since my brother Rubin, too, was still part of that pattern, and the trapped bird threw Rubin into a frenzy - I can only call it a frenzy, comrades - a frenzy of rage - or fear, maybe - I cannot say precisely - except that the sound of the struggling bird sent him wild - leaping for it, clutching at it, yelling, whimpering.... I had thought him frozen, where he lay, but at the first sound of the flapping wings he seemed to be on his feet, rushing round the cell, slipping, slithering, hitting the walls, trying to climb them, head turned upwards, arms above his head, fingers crooked, teeth bared. And as the bird looped lower, tiring, he jumped at it the wilder, frightening it, roaring it to a storm of panic.... Then the bird was gone, as suddenly as it came: it flew out, quite cleanly, through the bars, and everything was quiet again - and the loss of it, that bird, seemed to startle Rubin: he stood, looking up at the grille, then began to cry: he wrapped his arms around his head, slid down the cell wall to the floor, slowly, softly, settling, like a bag of water, it seemed, as if he had run to water - or sand - yes, sand, a loose bag of sand, settling, slowly, on the cell floor - and he cried, he sobbed - terrible, terrible sobs, that shook the whole flesh pool of him, there, on the stone floor, and I went to him and gathered him, as best I could, in my arms, and held him close, across my stomach, and he slept, quietly, for many hours, without resistance - to me or to his sleep - until the sun entered the cell for the fifty-fifth day, which

76

I did not mark, but continued to hold him, until he woke
and seemed restored, calmer.... He smiled for a
moment, and looked up at me ... I remember ... I had
decided that we must eat again and that, now, I must take
some initiative in the matter. So I layed Rubin back
against the wall, where he had fallen, beneath the window,
and took his collection of bones from his original place
and went to Lubianko's body where it lay, full length, at
the place of the remains, and, quite without emotion,
without hesitation, as I recall, I began to cut into the
flesh.... At first, comrades, I could not judge the
degree of pressure needed - the skin was surprisingly
strong and the cutting bone rather spoiled. Then I
recalled a phrase I had heard once from a surgeon - the
surgeon who amputated by turret-gunner's leg - last
winter, was it, or the winter before? - strange that it
should come to mind - 'If it needs cutting,' he said, 'then
it must be cut.' And I cut - clumsily - into Lubianko's
magnificent body.... But when I turned, to take food to
Rubin, I found him crouching in one corner of the cell,
his head on one side, grinning at me from behind his
beard - and when I moved towards him he started away,
along the wall, and then back again, darting, crouched
- and when I still came towards him, he screamed, he
raised his hands, palms outward, to fend me off - and I
had to leave the cut flesh on the cell floor in front of him.
Once more, he began to whimper, finally to cry, and
crying, let me hold him as before - I held him in my arms
- and I fed him, as I fed myself, on the flesh of our dead
brother ... then he slept. But this time he cried even in
his sleep, and when he woke, calmer for a moment, he
pulled himself away from me, pushed me to my own place
on the wall, and crouched in the corner, shoulders to the

77

cold stone, gibbering, moaning, his tongue lolling, saliva
sliding through his beard on to his chest.... Comrades,
it hurts me to talk thus of my brother, my dear brother
Rubin, whom I love, with whom I shared such torment
- Rubin, to whom I owe so much, who took upon himself
such burdens in our suffering. But I cannot pretend:
you have the testimony of the young lieutenant, Scriabin
- his sense of Rubin's state of mind at our release.
Doubtless the lieutenant told you how frightened he was,
how he clung to me. Oh, comrades, he held me round the
neck, his face pressed into my throat, and I couldn't
loosen him, couldn't lift him.... Your orderlies, too,
who washed him; your doctors, who had him bound and
drugged - they will have made their reports, their
diagnoses and prognoses: his spirit has been scalded
they will say, his mind has melted, he is berserk, he is
like an animal, he is mad!.... And you also, comrades
- in your pity - you will have seen Officer Rubin, lying,
like some waxwork, in his closed, white room. How,
then, can I suggest my brother is any other than as you
see him - as your doctors saw and heard him?... But
what, exactly, have they seen? What did they hear?
Stethoscopes, have they, for my brother Rubin's soul?
Which of them ever knew him, which could begin to
conceive the suffering that drove him (by their
categories) mad? Comrades, I grant them the conven-
ience of such categories: I only challenge their
foundation. And I challenge you, comrades - as judges:
I challenge your pity: you shelter in it. Rubin, too, has
a right to your judgement: he, too, awaits your decision
upon him: he, too, is in your hands. And what do you
know of him, comrades? Which of you, in all your pity,
have held him, as I held him, in my arms - held him,
78

comrades, naked to my nakedness, while his tears ran
down upon my cradling arms; held him, while he sobbed,
asleep; fed him, day by day, to the sixtieth day - fed him,
I say, and held him, and still did not know him, was
rejected by him, thrown aside, in terror, by him, and
held him again as he slept - and while he slept - yes,
comrades, while he slept - sharpened our brother
Lubianko's thighbone, silently, on the cell floor, to a
point, as a means of killing him?... I kept Rubin's own
collection of bones, his carving bones, away from him
- not out of fear, you understand - at that stage, there
was nothing to fear, with just the two of us, and
Lubianko lying dead - but it seemed a reasonable
precaution, in the circumstances - for I knew our present
situation could not last. Rubin knew it, too, as instinct,
somewhere within him - hence his moments of fright: it
was as if he had surrendered himself, but not completely
- and not completely to me. At some stage, when I could
no longer feed us, the pressures of thirst and hunger
would rise again, and I had no way of telling how those
pressures would affect him - nor how they might affect me.
All I knew (or thought I knew) was that, short of my own
suicide, or his - and short, of course, of our release
- violence between us, finally, was unavoidable....
Forgive me, comrades - I want to speak plainly. After
our long struggle for ... dignity, the dignified solution,
you might suggest - in your abstract sense - would have
been to choose death, together - an agreement to die
- before being forced to the last barbarity.... But
supposing, in the abstract sense, that you were right,
the dignified solution would have been, as it were,
impractical - because I judged my brother Rubin unable
to take a shared decision. The fact is, he no longer

heard what I said - and in those last days I spoke to him incessantly: why, I do not know, but I told him every-thing - all that I could summon of myself, my childhood, my parents, my marriage, my children, my wife - I told him about my wife, what we had done together, what we ate, what we read, even what we grew in our garden - I told him about our garden in Ryazan, the forests - I told him about Banishevsky, and my work, and the war, particularly the war - though he knew about the war - and, in any case, he wasn't listening.... If he could not hear my life, as I told it, I doubted he would hear suggestions as to death. Either he or I would commit suicide, separately, or one of us, at some point, would attack the other. It seemed a poor alternative, comrades, but I could anticipate nothing else: I had stopped hoping for release.... Yet the chance was not to be discounted - the chance of our being freed at any second. I did not expect it, hardly even wanted it, consciously, any more, but I did not discount the possibility. Therefore, it appeared to me, comrades, that, insofar as it lay in my control, I should stave off any resolution, between Rubin and myself, for as long as I could. And if the resolution was to be postponed, I felt it reasonable, too, to postpone any decision upon my own part in the matter.... Outside our dungeon, comrades, factors of the war, beyond our knowing, determined that we should be found at the sixtieth day, precisely - not the first day, as we might have wished, not at the hundredth day, when it would have been too late for all of us, not at the thousandth day or the ten thousandth, but at the sixtieth. Yet this was not the determinism of fate, comrades: I discuss nothing of fate - only factors of the war, only what happened.... And similarly, within our cell, any resolution, between
80

Rubin and myself, would have occurred at one certain point, amid many possible points, and that point, too, would have been determined by a whole series of related factors - the degree of our thirst, our hunger, for example, the state and focus of our minds, the condition of our bodies, the extent of our threat to each other ... changing factors, comrades - at some point they would have coalesced and precipitated a decision, and until that point, it seemed idle to speculate on what I might - or ought - to do.... Comrades, I have learned to distrust, somewhat, the decisions of philosophy - the provisional decisions, the tempting, moral gestures made before the act: too often, don't you find, the action distorts the philosophy - the philosophy, if you like, is premature? And then, sometimes, the philosophy distorts the action - wouldn't you agree? Altogether, I preferred to avoid the speculative, the decision on a merely beckoning situation: I preferred to trust myself: I preferred to make my decision when the time came - and until that time - until the crisis - if it came - I preferred to wait. I ask you to accept: what I wanted was to avoid doing anything at all, until action of some kind was unavoidable.... Yet, seeing little chance of escape, I also felt it reasonable to equip myself, as it were, for the alternative of violence - and therefore I cut out Lubianko's thighbone.... It never occurred to me to seek a weapon (for such it was) among the earlier remains: I took Lubianko's thighbone and sucked the marrow from it, as we always had - and Rubin, in a waking moment, saw me do it and smiled at me, I thought, indulgently - and I sharpened the bone as he slept - slowly, silently, on the cell floor I sharpened it - and considered with some objectivity its most effective

application - feeling, for instance, for my own heart, as
it pumped, beneath the fifth rib - and feeling my brother
Rubin's heart, beneath the thick hair of his chest, as he
lay in my arms ... until that sixtieth day, by my counting,
when your young lieutenant spared us.... Spared us
what? Comrades, he spared us our last confrontation....
Personally, I no longer feared death: I was resigned to
it, I say, yet resisting, for there still remained, I
thought, the better choice. And though it might seem
absurd to call life a choice, nonetheless, I chose it - I
still choose it ... I only feared that final resolution,
between my brother Rubin and myself - feared what it
would show me of myself - and him - of what we were....
But the revelation was averted by Lieutenant Scriabin.
Guess at it, if you will - I am content not to know myself
quite that far. I was lucky: Scriabin placed the judgement, comrades, upon you, assembled in this room:
since I have survived, you are required to judge. And
the facts of my survival are complete - all but for the
details of our release - which are painful to relate....
Rubin was terrified by the lieutenant's intrusion, by the
sound of the door cracking open, by the torchlight and its
disembodied voice - Scriabin's voice - asking 'Were we
his?' and later 'Could we walk?'... For Rubin, I would
say, the world, indeed, had shrunk to a vault of stone.
Hence his reaction to the little bird: there should have
been no bird: there should have been nothing but him and
me and that row of heads. And finally, I think, there was
nothing - nothing else - nothing, nowhere - only Rubin
and Vukhov, their carpet of blood and the pattern of their
torment - now seven, now six, five, four, three, now
two ... then the young lieutenant broke open the door and
the world rushed back into the vacuum.... For Rubin,

comrades, release was a dream, a nightmare: your
reality, the reality of his white, closed room, that, too,
is a nightmare: within him, as he lies there, now, he
waits the continuation of our suffering: it is all there
is.... And 'Could we walk?' asked the lieutenant. 'Oh
yes,' I said: we could walk: we were Rubin and Vukhov,
tank squadron, third assault brigade, and we had been
entombed for sixty days, without food, by the enemy, and
yes, yes, yes, we could walk.... And he left again,
young Scriabin - to fetch the two greatcoats - closing the
door behind him ... but the vile stench of us went with
him - up the stone steps with him and out into the summer
air of the monastery courtyard. And the young
lieutenant fell to his knees in the courtyard and vomited
- I heard it - he retched again and again, until it seemed
he would tear up his insides - and his men ran to him and
he recovered himself before them and stopped their
questions - about what he had found - and put a guard at
the stair top - am I not right, comrades? - and sent back
for the greatcoats.... And in the darkness, below, I
told Rubin we were free: in a great babble I told him - it
was over, at last, it was over, we had endured - his
child, he could see him again, and his old father - he'd
soon be the gymnast again - there was nothing more to
fear: in a babble I said it, but he could not hear, did
not want to hear ... and a second time, perhaps an hour
later, Scriabin came down the steps, having calmed and
steeled himself - and a second time he opened the cell
door - and retched - despite himself - was sick again,
leaning against the doorpost, his empty stomach turning
and turning, until he coughed and groaned and calmed
once more and switched on the torch and threw in the
coats - all of which frightened Rubin more than ever, so

that he scrambled out of my arms over into the farthest
corner and crouched there, whimpering, in the darkness.
The lieutenant followed him with the torch and Rubin fled
again, capering round the wall, and round, and the torch
followed him, until he tripped and fell over Lubianko's
body and rolled into the row of heads and screamed and
screamed as he lay there among the heads - frozen, in
terror. 'Please take the light off him,' I said - I
remember. And the young lieutenant - himself, perhaps,
rather frightened - switched off the torch. I crawled to
the greatcoats and pulled one on - heavy, rough, even to
my weathered skin - fastening each button, carefully, to
the throat.... But Rubin? What to do with Rubin? The
young lieutenant put on the torch again, shining it at me.
'What about him?' he said, gently, with great puzzlement.
Whatever his feelings - of horror, of disgust, of pity - I
sensed he was, so to speak, relying on me. 'Can you get
a coat over him?' he said. So I took the second greatcoat
and walked towards Officer Rubin - rather ludicrously, it
seems to me, now - holding the coat before me, like some
matador. Poor Rubin, he no longer knew me - and I - in
my greatcoat - hunting him - and the torch, following,
behind me.... All at once, he curled himself tight on the
floor, and when I knelt to him, opening out the coat, he
uncoiled, like a spring, at the last moment, and rolled
aside and up on to his haunches, and backwards, away,
along the wall. And I turned to the lieutenant - helpless,
shamed, and Scriabin said: 'We can't take him down like
that.' And, of course, comrades, I understood what he
meant: it was not merely a question of propriety: he
meant it was some distance down through the birch forest
- Rubin would have to be both covered and calmed: after
all, he was an officer, a major - hadn't I told the
84

lieutenant: Captain Vukhov, Major Rubin, the two last of
seven abandoned officers?... Naturally, I understood.
We could not be ignored: we could not simply be left
there - in our cell - whatever the lieutenant might
privately have wished. Nor could he deal summarily with
us, as it were, since I, at least, was so ... composed
.... Consider, comrades: might not the easiest thing
have been for Scriabin to use his pistol on us - to put us
down - then to shut the door upon us, as if our awful
history had never happened - and to destroy the building,
to wipe out all trace of us, of our torment?... But it was
too late, comrades: the time for hygiene (if you will
forgive the phrase) was when the young lieutenant first
found us - and my rationality prevented it. Now Scriabin
had sent for the greatcoats: his men had seen him
vomiting, had questioned him: it was too late for simple
measures.... 'Try this,' he said, as I knelt, confused,
on the cell floor. And when I went to him, slowly,
hesitantly, where he stood, in the doorway - aghast, yet
fascinated - when I went to him, I say, he gave me a
cloth soaked in chloroform.... Yes, comrades, Scriabin,
too, had understood - he is a clever young man: he had
sent back for chloroform to calm Rubin, as well as a
greatcoat to cover him - and I was now to quell my dear
brother, whom I had nursed and fed, whom I loved more
than any other living thing, whom I had loved almost unto
death.... But how was it to be done, except forcibly?
The lieutenant would not enter the cell, would not pass
the doorpost, would not help.... I resolved that there
was no alternative. To be sure, I regret it now. But in
my regret, comrades, the difficult question remains: was
there another way? I cannot tell.... At the time, in all
the shock, new considerations were weighing upon me

- Scriabin's considerations: could they be ignored? I, too, was breathing unfamiliar air - the air of the great outside, the summer air, simmering, at the top of the steps. I saw no alternative to supressing Rubin - he was so frightened, so withdrawn: he no longer remembered he wanted to be free: he would struggle, I thought, even at my coaxing.... Comrades, I had tried to coax him, tried to prepare him, while the lieutenant went for the coats - and the chloroform. I had tried to tell him there was nothing, now, to fear.... How absurd! Nothing to fear! And here I was, moving upon him, not with Lubianko's sharpened thighbone but with an army great-coat - trying to deceive him with calm words, thinking to press the cloth to his face, suddenly, when I was near to him, hoping he would trust me so that I could betray his trust - for his own good, I told myself - rather for mine! And when he wouldn't trust me, but still edged away from me, along the wall, then I rushed at him and threw the coat over him and caught him under it and felt for his head and held it, by the hair, as he twisted and fought and bit and scratched: I held my brother Rubin, not as he had held our companion, Lubianko, but with the clumsiness of uncertainty, of doubt, once more of shame - and I pressed the cloth to his mouth and straddled him, strong as he was, until he was still and quiet, and then I wrapped him in the coat - I notice that fact now, comrades - I did not dress him in the coat but wrapped him in it, wrapped him round and buttoned it to the throat and tried to lift him but couldn't and so had to drag him across the cell because the lieutenant, for his own reasons, would not cross the threshhold.... I dragged my unconscious brother Rubin across our cell, I say, and half raised him, for the lieutenant to lift, and watched the lieutenant carry him
86

up the steps ahead of me, and picked up Lubianko's thighbone from my place on the wall and put it in my sleeve
- as memento, you might say - as witness - my silent
witness. Then I followed Scriabin up the worn steps and
outside, into the gathering dawn, which dazzled me, so
that I stumbled and fell. And no one came to help me.
Instead, the watching soldier-squad moved back from us
and Scriabin had to demand help from them - someone to
take Rubin's legs.... Comrades, his men had already
made rough stretchers for us - both of us - and four of
the squad were detailed to carry us down through the
birch forest, with two more as escort - while behind us,
the resourceful lieutenant laid his explosive in the
monastery ruins.... On his own initiative, comrades,
Scriabin had decided what must be done - what was best
- and besides the greatcoats (officers' greatcoats) and
the chloroform and the stretchers, he had ordered
dynamite.... Behind us, all at once, there were six,
perhaps seven explosions, some muffled, some clear, and,
way below, on the hillside, as we were, dust and ...
debris filtered down upon us through the leaves....
Comrades, there is no escape, it seems to me, from what
has happened. Already, on that journey from the razed
monastery, I knew that my release was purely provisional.
In the close confines of our four walls I had begun to
consider the freedom of release as absolute, my future
vast and uncontained.... I beg you, comrades, try to
grasp the circumstances which produced so childish an
illusion.... Now, in the faces of my bearers, I
recognised my error: I saw repulsion, I saw disgust.
Those soldiers said nothing, not a word, but their eyes,
their faces, they were your eyes, comrades, and your
faces, as I first stood here before you - and from them I

87

knew that, despite himself, the young lieutenant must
have told what he had seen. Perhaps, as he knelt,
vomiting, on the courtyard cobbles, and his men rushed
to him, perhaps he said: 'They've been eating each
other,' or perhaps 'Oh God, they've been eating each
other.' Whatever he said, and however quickly he
recovered himself, however efficiently he otherwise
dealt with the situation, it was enough.... I do not
blame him. I ask myself: could I have stayed silent at
such a time, after such a sight? And I think not: words,
I would say, are an excusable recourse at moments of
such anguish.... Nonetheless, comrades, taking my own
part, I ask you, imagine: to have been named
(inadvertently perhaps, yet to have been named) cannibal
- cannibal, comrades - devourer of my brothers' flesh
- and then to be seen smiling at the scent of the birch
trees on that downward journey through the forest, to be
seen smiling while my brother Rubin lay bound, in his
greatcoat, unconscious - insane.... Why was I not
distraught, like him? Who, or rather, what was I, to
walk, composed, from such a torment? In that forest
journey, comrades, I foresaw this very hearing - the
need of it - on your behalf - and mine: I saw this
hearing, forgive me, as the price of my freedom:
having endured my torment, I saw that I should have to
explain that endurance. How were we still alive at the
sixtieth day, Rubin and I? What had happened to Rubin,
to hurt him so? What had happened to the five other
officers whom you must have listed as missing?... Such
stories may perhaps be hid when no one endures to tell
them. But I, Vukhov, I comrades, am the man who came
through: I know what occurred at the monastery of
St. Peter Rabinovich and I am able to recount it

88

- therefore I am required to recount it - and therefore I
am under your judgement for being able to recount it.
Isn't that the case, comrades? I am on trial, as it were,
for my rationality - and rightly so, reasonably so. My
regret is that the telling of my story should involve such
pain - to you, comrades, I think - and more particularly,
to the families of my dear cell-brothers. I can only ask
forgiveness: there was nothing else to be done - I saw
that, on the journey through the forest: I foresaw the
need to defend myself - a prospect I had never once
envisaged in our cell: in some degree, I even saw the
pattern of my defence, the shape of this, my testimony,
my rehearsal of the facts.... And my defence, comrades,
is now complete. Had things turned out otherwise, I
would plead with you to let me nurse my brother Rubin
- to let me stay with him, to hold him, feed him, talk to
him, restore him, if you like, to your reality. It would
be my duty, would it not? It would be my love. Who
could help him more than I, Vukhov, partner in his
suffering?... Anyone, comrades! The answer must be:
anyone! Anyone could help him more than I! In his sleep,
it is possible, I still hunt him, with that spread greatcoat,
like some matador: waking, he could only fear me - fear
me more than anyone - me, who suppressed him, like an
animal, and delivered him to your doctors, who have
bound him and pronounced him mad. Mad, comrades!
Mad! Your categories! My brother Rubin is as sane as
any man among us to be left distraught by such an agony!
... But your doctors disagree. So I must beg you to
care for him instead - to grant him your most constant
and most patient care. Naturally, you will treat him by
your rules, but I beg you, do not forget that he is still
himself, whatever has been made of him - and that time

may yet soften the agony of being himself. I trust there will always be that hope for him, at least. Therefore, please, within your rules, preserve the chance of his waking - encourage him to wake - to reawaken - to your ... reality.... For myself, comrades, I beg nothing. I thank you for your courtesy in hearing my defence and leave to you the larger implications of my narrative - the matter of some protest to the enemy, the obsolescence of present conventions governing the conduct of the war.... For myself, I say, I submit to your judgement. By your categories, I hope, I am sane enough to be judged - though by my dear Rubin's example that might make me mad - and you mad with me - on the rough resemblance of our rationalities.... For the purpose of this hearing, I ask only that you accept me as man among you, and to accept, nevertheless, that we are all different men - we here, assembled in this room - and all act differently in our mingled histories.... Tomorrow, should my brother Rubin wake and meet your categories of normalcy, wouldn't you perhaps declare him purged by what you term his madness? What, then, of me? Forgive me, I require no purgation. If I am in any sense guilty in this case, then so must Rubin be, whom you pity. Of what can I be guilty that he is not? Certainly we are guilty - both of us! But of what?... Determine the nature of my guilt and I bow readily to whatever punishment or remedy you may propose. Should you judge yourselves incompetent so to determine, I ask only to be returned to the theatre of the war.... What have I done, comrades, and what has been done to me, that I should expect some safe conduct from hostilities? The war is far from over: it shows scant sign of abating. If I am not judged unfit, by reason of my experience, I have the right of active service, the right of return to arms. That is my choice: it is where I belong: my torment itself, I say, was but an episode of war.... Of course, comrades, in describing it, in detailing the long weeks of my suffering, I have been tempted to ask: 'Why me?' The question, I think, is not entirely rhetorical: the correct reply, I suggest, is: 'Why not me?' At all events, that is the reply I prefer.... Your problem, I take it, is what shall be done with me. I am content the question is not purely mine.... Comrades, this, my defence, is my history - and my history, like it or not, is what occurred. What, then, will you do with me? Comrades, I await your judgement. Comrades, I say, what is to be done with me? What is to be done?